HEROES IN MY HEAD

Also by Judy Rebick

Politically Speaking (with Kiké Roach)
Imagine Democracy
Ten Thousand Roses: The Making of a Feminist Revolution
Transforming Power: From the Personal to the Political
Occupy This!

HEROES IN MY HEAD

A MEMOIR

JUDY REBICK

ANANSI

Published in Canada in 2018 by House of Anansi Press Inc.
www.houseofanansi.com

House of Anansi Press is committed to protecting our natural environment.
As part of our efforts, the interior of this book is printed on paper that contains 100%
post-consumer recycled fibres, is acid-free, and is processed chlorine-free.

22 21 20 19 18 1 2 3 4 5

Library and Archives Canada Cataloguing in Publication

Rebick, Judy, author
Heroes in my head : a memoir / Judy Rebick.

Issued in print and electronic formats.
ISBN 978-1-4870-0357-9 (SOFTCOVER). — ISBN 978-1-4870-0358-6
(EPUB). — ISBN 978-1-4870-0359-3 (MOBI)

1. Rebick, Judy. 2. National Action Committee on the
Status of Women—Presidents—Biography. 3. Feminists—Canada—
Biography. 4. Women social reformers—Canada—Biography.
5. Pro-choice movement—Canada. 6. Autobiographies. I. Title.

HQ1455.R43 A3 2018 305.42092 C2017-904743-4
C2017-904744-2

Book design: Alysia Shewchuk

*We acknowledge for their financial support of our publishing program
the Canada Council for the Arts, the Ontario Arts Council, and the Government of
Canada through the Canada Book Fund.*

Printed and bound in Canada

MIX
Paper from
responsible sources
FSC® C004071

To my brothers

CONTENTS

AUTHOR'S NOTE

AS THE EDITING OF THIS BOOK was coming to an end, the #metoo movement started. Women spoke out about the sexual harassment and abuse they suffered at the hands of powerful men, raising the movement against gendered violence and misogyny to a massive level. This book is my #metoo. I wanted to tell my secrets before #metoo, but the movement has deepened my belief that our secrets are killing us and telling our secrets is a liberating act for us and for others. My hope is that my story will contribute to making the #metoo movement stronger and more inclusive because I think childhood sexual abuse at the hands of a family member is much more widespread than we are led to believe. The growing movement against patriarchy must include this issue, too.

In my sixties, when my short-term memory was starting to fail, I complained at a family gathering about ageing.

"Let's face it, Judy," said my niece Kael, "memory was never your strong suit." Indeed as you will learn in these pages, my memory of my life has huge gaps. So how do I write a memoir? I interviewed a lot of people who remembered what I didn't; I have kept the journals from those decades; and for the public aspects of my life, I reviewed clippings and videos. Memory is subjective, and this book represents my memories.

Some of the names in the book have been changed or I've used first names only. Just because I've decided to tell my secrets doesn't mean everyone else in my life has. Most of the dialogue is constructed as closely as possible to my memories of the events. I suspect even those with excellent memory don't remember every word of a discussion.

The language reflects the time, so words like "crippled" or "Indian" are used as they were in those days. I also use the term "multiple personality disorder" because that was the diagnostic term used at the time. "Dissociative identity disorder" is the term used today. I think "multiple personality disorder" better describes my experience. I've tried to explain those instances where I use slang from the sixties and seventies.

what is stronger
than the human heart
which shatters over and over
and still lives

—Rupi Kaur, *Milk and Honey*

The soul of feminist politics is the commitment to ending patriarchal domination of women and men, girls and boys. Love cannot exist in any relationship that is based on domination and coercion.

—bell hooks, *The Will to Change:
Men, Masculinity, and Love*

Prologue

WARRIOR WOMAN

ON JUNE 15, 1983, Dr. Henry Morgentaler opened an illegal abortion clinic in Toronto. The Ontario Coalition for Abortion Clinics (OCAC) had chosen a spot on the second floor of a lovely Victorian house on Harbord Street, a quiet downtown thoroughfare lined with bookstores and cafés near the University of Toronto. With the Toronto Women's Bookstore on the ground floor, we were assured of supportive neighbours. The interior staircase up to the clinic was useful for security purposes—if anyone broke in, it gave the nurses and doctors time to secure the patients—and there was a front stoop, perfect for rallies. The plan was to hold a symbolic opening for the media at 10 a.m. Dr. Morgentaler, who lived in Montreal, would arrive at 3 p.m., say a few words, and then go inside.

OCAC had convinced Dr. Morgentaler to open a clinic in Toronto to repeat the success he had had with his clinic in

Montreal. After three jury acquittals, the Parti Québécois government declared they would no longer prosecute a doctor for conducting abortions under safe conditions — in essence legalizing abortion in Quebec. Criminal law is decided at the federal level in Canada, but the provinces are charged with enforcing the law. Quebec would no longer enforce the restrictive abortion law, which forced a woman to appear before a Therapeutic Abortion Committee (TAC) of three doctors who would decide if her life or health was at stake. Since hospitals were not required to have TACs, the largely Catholic hospitals in Quebec provided little access to abortions.

Dr. Morgentaler had asked me to be the spokesperson for the clinic, so at 10 a.m. I unlocked the door. Some of the media had already shown up, and more and more were arriving. The clinic staff were there and a few members of OCAC were outside.

"Can you walk up the steps and unlock the door for us, Judy?" a camera guy asked.

"Sure."

As soon as I opened the door, another camera crew arrived.

"Can you do it again?" they asked, again and again.

As the time of the doctor's arrival drew near, there were close to a hundred people from the media — print, TV, and radio reporters, camerapeople, photographers — standing on the sidewalk and spilling onto the street.

We didn't expect any trouble that day. Toronto Right to Life, the local anti-abortion organization, had announced that they would not hold a protest; instead they would rely on the Conservative government, then in power in Ontario, to shut down the illegal clinic. Just in case, we had organized a small rally of supporters.

When Dr. Morgentaler arrived, Cheryl, a calm and rational psychiatric nurse, and I were waiting to escort him to the clinic.

"Bit of a crazy scene with all the media, Henry," I said as he stepped out of the cab.

"To be expected." He laughed.

Cheryl was behind him on his left side, and I was on his right side, a few steps in front. A white van stopped to let us pass. As I turned to thank the driver, a short but sturdy middle-aged man violently grabbed Dr. Morgentaler's arm. I stepped between him and the doctor and pulled his hands away, while Cheryl hurried Dr. Morgentaler into the clinic.

"Get out of here!" I said, pushing him away with one hand on his arm and the other on his chest. "What the hell do you think you're doing?"

"Go away," he said in heavily accented English.

Then he raised his arm and I blocked his arm with mine. That's when I realized he had garden shears. He looked me in the eyes and put his arm down.

"I'm not going anywhere," I replied. "You better get out of here and fast."

He started to walk away and I was following him when I heard Cheryl, who had come back out and was running down the street, yelling my name: "Judy, stop!"

Her voice sounded very far away, but the urgency in her tone pulled me back to the present. I suddenly realized it was crazy to chase down the man. Dr. Morgentaler was safe; now we could leave it to the police.

That night I was staying with my old friend Susan Swan. I had met Susan two decades earlier at McGill University, where we both worked on the *McGill Daily* student newspaper. The week the clinic opened, she had broken up with her boyfriend and wanted company. I remember we were watching the news together. The clinic opening was the lead story, and footage of Morgentaler's arrival played out on national TV. It was only then that I became fully aware that the attacker had raised the garden shears against Dr. Morgentaler.

The phone rang. It was Henry.

"Judy, I wish to thank you for saving my life." Only when he saw the news coverage did he, too, realize that I had put myself in harm's way to save him.

"I don't think he wanted to kill you, Henry, but you're welcome," I said with a little chuckle. At that moment, I was still feeling quite relaxed.

That changed the next day. As soon as I woke up, all I could think was *I have to go home, I have to go home*. I realized something was wrong so I called my therapist at the time, Mark Smith. He hadn't seen the news so I told him what had happened the day before.

"You're in shock, Judy," he said. "Even though you didn't realize it at the time, you were traumatized by the violence and now you are in shock." We talked some more and I started to cry. I wound up crying for more than an hour and called in sick to work, taking the day to recover.

The "garden shears attack," as it has come to be known, has forever defined the pro-choice battle in Canada. A video clip of the confrontation is played on TV every time Dr.

Morgentaler or the pro-choice struggle is mentioned. It was the beginning of an intense struggle on the streets, in the media, and in the courts, culminating in the 1988 Supreme Court decision that made abortion legal in Canada, a victory that even the right-wing government of Stephen Harper was unable to challenge. It was also when my public image as a warrior for women's rights was established both in the public's eyes and in my own.

I knew that cool, fearless woman who stopped the attack on Dr. Morgentaler: she had been protecting me for years. But it would take longer for me to understand who she was and why she existed than it would to make abortion legal in Canada.

The secret stayed buried for decades, through a clinical depression, several relationships, illness and injuries, world travel, and a life of activism. Here and there an image, a feeling, a shadow, a gap in time would appear only to be quickly relegated to that part of my brain that was separated from my consciousness by a concrete wall. Decades later, a tiny detail put a crack in the wall and before long it came tumbling down.

I

EVERYTHING FALLS APART

1989

One

THE WALL COMES DOWN

IN EARLY JULY 1989, I got a call at work from Clayton Ruby, a progressive lawyer in Toronto. I'd known Clayton for more than a decade. In 1972, he and his business partner at the time, Paul Copeland, had defended Grass Roots, a radical youth group that had occupied a piece of land at the University of Toronto to set up a tent city for transient youth. Twenty-one people were arrested.

"I'm working on the Barbara Dodd case and I need your help," he said.

Of course I knew about the Barbara Dodd case. Her ex-boyfriend, Gregory Murphy, had sought an injunction to stop her from having an abortion. A year and a half before, on January 28, 1988, the Supreme Court of Canada had ruled that the law criminalizing abortion was unconstitutional. The procedure was now legal in Canada. But on July 5, 1989, Ontario Court justice John O'Driscoll, who was known for his anti-abortion views, made Dodd's fetus a ward of the court, halting her scheduled procedure at Women's College Hospital. The Ontario Coalition for Abortion Clinics called O'Driscoll's decision "judicial terrorism" and demanded that the attorney general appeal the dangerous precedent. Dodd's sister, Liz Dodd, hired Ruby to appeal the decision on Barbara's behalf.

Barbara Dodd was also deaf.

Two days later, a Montreal judge awarded an injunction to Jean-Guy Tremblay, the ex-boyfriend of a woman named Chantal Daigle, to stop her from having an abortion. The Supreme Court victory legalizing abortion was being challenged in the country's two biggest provinces. From the time of the opening of the Morgentaler clinic on June 15, 1983, I had helped to lead an intense battle not only with the ferocious anti-abortion militants but with the government, the courts, and the police. I was fully my warrior self, battling with the forces of evil, on the side of justice not only on the abortion issue but also in my paid work at the Canadian Hearing Society (CHS). Deaf people were just starting to organize, and my job as director of special projects was to support them. On May 12, 1989, we held a rally in front of the legislature calling for American Sign Language (ASL) to be used in schools for the deaf. We were victorious in both battles. I was feeling pretty good.

"You know how to use sign language, right?" Clayton asked.

"Yes." I hesitated. "But I'm not a qualified interpreter." One of my jobs at CHS had been to set up the Ontario Interpreter Services, which was the first professional agency for sign language interpreters in the country. CHS was working to make sure sign language interpreters were treated by the courts with the same professional standards as other language interpreters. Before the establishment of the Ontario Interpreter Services, there was no way to officially recognize the qualifications of sign language interpreters. My sign language was good, but not good enough to act as an interpreter. Even though I had stopped working with OCAC in the summer of 1987, I was always hesitant to advocate on behalf of an individual on an issue in which I was involved as an activist. Individuals are highly unpredictable, especially when under pressure, and you can risk your public credibility on the issue itself if things go wrong.

"I don't need you to interpret. The court is hiring an interpreter. I just need someone to sit with Barbara and explain to her what's happening in court, answer her questions, maybe help me to communicate with her. You'd be perfect. Please."

"I don't know, Clay. You know I'm not involved with OCAC anymore."

"You'd be there as an assistant from the CHS, not as an activist."

"I don't think my boss would go along with that."

"Would you ask him? I really need you. It's important."

Sinking in my chair, I agreed to ask Denis, hoping he would say no. Denis Morrice was an amazing boss. In 1975, he had taken over a sleepy agency that served deaf and hard of hearing people. As executive director, he had turned CHS into a vibrant and effective organization. Recognizing my contribution to the agency, as well as my commitment to political activism, Denis pretty well gave me as much time off as I needed for my activist work. As a political activist, I was an experienced change maker and Denis understood how to use those skills to improve services for deaf and hard of hearing people. Not only had I led efforts in establishing Ontario Interpreter Services, but I had worked with builders in constructing CHS's new offices; helped to win a CRTC case against Bell Canada, forcing the company to provide a message-relay service for the deaf; co-chaired a coalition for employment equity for people with disabilities; and now was assisting deaf people in their fight to get American Sign Language taught in Ontario schools for the deaf, where they had always refused to teach ASL even though that was how most deaf people communicated. He didn't want me to quit.

Still, I was surprised that Denis liked the idea of my assisting Barbara Dodd. My pro-choice activism had caused a lot of trouble for him. At the time the issue was very controversial, and anti-abortion staff and board members had tried to get me fired. But he saw the Barbara Dodd case as a way that CHS could legitimately support my pro-choice work. CHS's mandate was to assist deaf people and Barbara needed my assistance.

When I met Barbara in Clayton's office just before the hearing, I immediately felt uneasy. Most deaf people who communicate in ASL are very direct. Despite her friendliness and charm, Barbara seemed guarded. Nevertheless I sat with her in court and answered her questions. After the hearing she asked me to refer her for an abortion should she win her case. I told her what I told any woman: to contact the Women's Health Referral line.

On July 13, Clayton convinced the appeal judge to overturn the injunction. The first post–Supreme Court challenge to abortion rights had been successfully defeated. The pro-choice movement had scored another victory. Dodd told the *Toronto Star*, "This is my decision. I decided what I want and he [her boyfriend] has no right to control my life or my body."

The court case ended on a Thursday and on Friday I headed up to Muskoka to spend the weekend at my friends' cottage along with my sixteen-year-old niece Kael, who was staying with me that summer. Lying on the dock, feeling the sun warm my body, looking out onto the familiar landscape of pine trees almost touching the water, I was awash with a rare feeling of peace.

Later that evening I checked my answering machine at home. There was an urgent message from Clayton.

"Have you seen the news?" he asked. Barbara Dodd had turned. She had had the abortion at Morgentaler's Toronto clinic, but her ex-boyfriend convinced her that she had made a mistake.

"She's blaming the women's movement for pressuring her to have it," Clayton said. "You have to come back. *The Journal* wants to do a feature this week. It's better for you to deal with this." *The Journal* was the magazine section of CBC TV News and hosted by famed journalist Barbara Frum.

When I got back to Toronto, I called Liz Dodd to find out what had happened. She was extremely agitated. "He's taken control of her mind. It's not her, Judy. I know my sister and it's not her. He's taken over her mind."

I tried to calm her. "Sometimes women are vulnerable

after a procedure. And Barbara has been under more pressure than most because of the court and the media attention. No doubt the anti-choice people have been pressuring her, too."

"No, it's him. He's evil. He's taken control of her," she insisted. It was a very disturbing conversation. It wasn't just that Barbara seemed to have changed her mind — that wasn't so surprising to me. There was something about Liz saying that Barbara's boyfriend had taken control of her mind. That phrase kept repeating over and over again in my brain: "He's taken control of her mind."

A few hours later, I turned on the news. Dodd and Murphy had held a press conference; the media had also caught the action outside the building: Liz Dodd was yelling at Murphy and was even more agitated than she had been on the phone. An officer was trying to calm her down, but she pushed him away. Then he grabbed her and forced her into the police car.

A torrent of images suddenly flooded my mind. A well-dressed man. A little girl lying on a bed. He's touching her, getting her to touch him. I don't see his face. *Not right, not right, not right. Who is he? What's happening? What is this about?* I had once seen this image while in my therapist's office but it was a brief flash, almost like a waking dream. Now there were multiple images of a little girl and a grown man. I lost touch with my surroundings and started to moan.

A couple of days later, I made an appointment with Marcia Weiner, a psychologist specializing in treating adults who had experienced sexual abuse. She was in her late fifties, more than ten years older than me. I knew her from the women's movement and I trusted her.

Marcia's office was in a high-rise condo overlooking the Don Valley, with a beautiful view of the Don River. I sat down in the small waiting room in the entrance to the apartment.

Marcia greeted me with a big smile, then led me into her office, which was calm, comforting, and filled with light. She sat in an easy chair on one side of a coffee table; I sat on the other side. We talked a bit about her practice.

"I started out being interested in women's sexual dysfunction," she explained. "But it soon became apparent that many women who had sexual and relational issues also had a history of childhood sexual abuse."

"I don't have sexual dysfunction," I insisted. I was convinced my dysfunction was more emotional than sexual. "A few years ago, I was in therapy. I was going through a clinical depression, which is why I was seeing the therapist. It cost me my only long-term relationship. I haven't had a relationship since then, that's true, but I'm just too busy. You know how busy I am.

"It was only at the end of therapy that I had some idea that I'd been abused. Now I have all these memories and I don't know what they are. A man is touching me, getting me to touch him, but I don't know who he is."

"Okay, let's not worry about that now. We'll concentrate on the memory you just had. When was that?"

"Last week, I called you right away," I said. "I've been trying to figure out who it could be. My aunt got an annulment around that time, so I'm thinking maybe it was her husband and my parents found out so she got rid of him. But why wouldn't anyone tell me once I was an adult? To tell you the truth, I'm having trouble thinking about anything else."

"It's very common to forget, especially if sexual abuse is severe or by someone close to you," Marcia explained. "Forgetting is a way of surviving."

Not me, I don't forget difficult things. I face them squarely, I thought. Yet I was more forgetful than most people. There were whole periods of my life that I couldn't remember.

"Trying to remember probably won't work, but one of the ways that is often helpful is through hypnosis. I suggest we try it at the next session."

As soon as I arrived for my next session, Marcia confirmed that I still wanted to proceed and then began. She asked me to lie down on the sofa and then to slowly breathe in and out. Once I was relaxed she said, "Think of a place you feel safe."

I imagined I was on a small beach looking out at calm blue lake water. It was quiet except for the gentle lapping of the waves.

"Now count down from one hundred."

As I counted down, my voice was becoming more distant and I started to feel like I was outside my body.

When I got to eighty-five, Marcia said, "I want you to imagine you're looking at the image you saw in your memory but on a TV screen. It's a little blurred. Adjust the image to make it clearer. What do you see?"

At first the screen was very blurry, even blurrier than the actual memory. I reached over to the imaginary TV and fiddled with the dial. "We're in the apartment in the basement of Grandma's house. It's very dark. There's only one window and it's high, too high for me to reach even when I stand on the bed. I'm in my bed and he is standing over me...Oh my god, it's my father...That can't be. How can that be?" Oddly, I wasn't feeling anything; I was calm, almost numb.

"Take a breath," she said. "Just tell me what you see. You are looking at it on TV. He can't hurt you now."

"He's standing over me. He's putting my hand on his penis. I'm pulling my hand away." I shook my head. I was starting to shake. I turned my head away.

"That's good, Judy. Let's leave it there. You've done a great job." She had me count up to get out of the hypnotic state. "Most people don't get this far in the first session. How are you feeling?"

"I don't know how I'm feeling. I can't believe it's my father. Why wouldn't I remember that? My father? He was violent and domineering. I remember that. But why wouldn't I remember being abused? Are you sure this is right?"

I knew the location though, the basement of my grandmother's house in Brooklyn, where we lived before I was five years old. I was young, so young. No adult male except my father came into the room when I was in bed. My uncle Sol would always see me upstairs at my grandma's house. My grandfather never came down either.

"We'll see as we go along. This was just the first session. It's unlikely you would see your father if it wasn't your father, but time will tell."

THE NEXT WEEK, we went back to the TV screen, and over several sessions the picture and the story became clearer.

At first it was more feelings than memories that were emerging. But as the memories emerged, I was beginning to experience emotions that were overwhelming. Marcia explained that for a child these emotions were unbearable, but for an adult, with help and at a certain distance from the events, it was possible to bear them.

Shortly after my first few sessions with Marcia, I went to see Kristi Magraw, a massage therapist who had been treating me for years. Kristi had developed her own style of massage, the Magraw Method, which was designed to release emotions through bodywork. Her work helped get me to the point where I was starting to uncover some of the feelings that my physical and emotional armour had been keeping from me.

I remember feeling a green slime slithering like a snake out of my body. It moved up from my lower bowel into my intestines, my stomach, and then out of my mouth.

"I think I'm going to be sick," I told Kristi in a panic. I started to get off the table.

"You're safe here. I've got a bucket," she said.

She continued to gently massage me.

"What is this?" I asked her. "What's going on?"

"What does it feel like?"

"Like my body is full of green slime. My whole digestive tract is full of green slime; it's coming up into my mouth. It's horrible."

"Can you identify a feeling?

After a moment, a word came into my head: "Shame."

It was shame. I was sick with shame.

Two

WHERE'S JACK?

"WHERE'S JACK?" THE VOICE asked. The words came from my mouth, but I, Judy, did not speak them.

"Jack's not here," Marcia responded calmly. "Who is asking?"

To my great surprise, the voice answered, "My name is Simon."

"Hello, Simon, welcome," Marcia said. "What do you want to talk about?"

"I'm glad Judy came to see you. I think you can help her. But I've been thinking...you should know about us."

"Thank you, Simon. I appreciate that. There are others?"

"Yes. But they're still afraid. Not sure it's safe. They worry about Jack, Judy's father. We haven't seen him in a while but the little ones are still worried about him. And some of them don't trust *you*, either. But I do. You seem kind. I think you're trying your best to help."

"Thanks for trusting me, Simon. I want to help Judy. That's why she came here. You're right that I'll be able to help her better if I know more about you and the others."

I could hear them but I couldn't speak. It was like Simon was occupying my body and part of my psyche, and I was somewhere in a corner of my mind where I could hear and see but not speak or act.

"Can I talk to Judy now, please?" Marcia asked. Simon quietly disappeared, like a vivid dream that vanishes the instant you wake up.

"Judy?"

"Yes," I said. "Can you tell it's me?"

"Yes, I can. Do you understand what just happened?"

"No, not really."

"Have you ever heard voices in your head that seemed different from your own?"

I hesitated but I figured I had to tell her everything.

"At a certain point in my therapy with Mark, an angry male voice emerged from deep inside me. I didn't seem to be controlling it but I could hear it. Mark explained that it was quite common in people who were burying a part of themselves."

We started talking more about the history of my sexual relationships. My sexual relationships weren't something I thought about a lot, which I knew made me different from most women. I remembered that I didn't date as a teenager after my father humiliated the first boy to take me out on a date. By the time I was eighteen, I gained a lot of weight and put my lack of a love life down to my weight gain. When I was in university, I got involved with Roger, an older man who had an important impact on my life even though the relationship lasted only a year. After that, I always had a boyfriend until my breakup with Ken Theobald, with whom I had lived for more than five years. I hadn't had a serious relationship since then. That was seven years ago, the same time I got intensely involved in the women's movement and wasn't meeting as many men. I did have a number of sexual liaisons, but I didn't think much about them. I had completely forgotten about some of them.

"These memory losses, especially around relationships, are a form of dissociation. For example, if a young child is continually abused at home or in school one of the ways of dealing with this is to 'forget,' (i.e., dissociate). The forgetting enables the child to function day to day without fear, shame, grief, or anger. The child looks 'normal' to the outside world. If the abuse were to stay in the memory, the child might not be able to deal with the feelings and knowledge, becoming so overwhelmed that she could attempt to end her life or she could become so totally disorganized in her thinking that she'd be seen as 'psychotic,'" Marcia explained. "You dissociated as a way of surviving the abuse and then you developed a habit of doing it when something threatened you. What often happens is that little Judy forgets the abuse when she awakes and goes to breakfast with her family. But she may start to 'remember' late at night when she hears footsteps approaching her bed. However, the part that 'remembers' isn't daytime Judy but another 'part' or 'alter' personality which experiences the abuse and only comes out when she is similarly threatened."

"But I remember having sex with some men but not with others. I don't get it."

"For now the details aren't important. I just want you to understand the process. You realized in therapy with Mark that you had buried your feelings over time. That's often because of dissociation. Dissociation is really very common. Think about a long drive when you are alone, and suddenly you realize you're not sure where you are or how you got there. You dissociated, departed from yourself out of boredom. Or a moment of trauma where you feel you're outside your body, observing yourself and the situation. This is another kind of dissociation.

"Now it seems that you have alter personalities, another more extreme form of dissociation. Usually when the alter personality emerges, you won't remember what happens. Have you heard about multiple personality disorder?"

"Sure, *The Three Faces of Eve*, *Sybil*. I've heard about it. But I doubt I have multiple personalities. I'm not crazy. No one has ever said anything about erratic behaviour or anything like that."

"MPD is not 'crazy' at all. It's actually a way of avoiding 'going crazy,'" Marcia replied. "Simon says there are others. They should start coming out now; we shall see. Multiple personality disorder presents differently in each person. As therapy continues, we'll have a better idea of how it has affected you. How are you feeling about it?"

"I'm not sure. It's kind of weird but somehow I feel relieved. Does that make sense?"

"Sure it does. You've had some inkling of other voices in your conscious mind from time to time."

"The Voice was always angry. This one seems quite nice...Simon, I wonder if that comes from Simon Says. That's funny."

"He's probably the guardian personality. There is usually a guardian personality who takes care of all the alters. Simon knows about the others. Some of the alters know about the others and some don't. It makes sense that he would come out first and decide if it's safe for the others."

Part of me was fascinated and part of me was horrified. Ever since the depression I'd known I was damaged by something, but multiple personalities? I wasn't crazy. I was one of the most functional people I knew. I trusted Marcia, but still, I should have challenged her. I should have gone to the library and read everything there was on multiple personalities to arm myself with arguments.

Yet I didn't do any of that. I went home and continued my life as if nothing had changed. I didn't even tell anyone about it. How could I? What would I say? I put it aside, as I had put so many things aside.

But I did start thinking about my childhood, about what I remembered that could reinforce or contradict these memories that were emerging.

II

MEMORIES ARE MADE OF THIS

1945–1970

Three

FAMILY TIES

I HAVE TWO TINY black-and-white framed photos on my bookshelf. Both pictures have the same background: my maternal grandmother's house in Brooklyn, where everything began. The first one used to sit on my grandma's mantelpiece. Grandma Bessie Schutter was a stout woman with a Russian peasant's body, buxom with ample hips. Her wide, kind face was surrounded by curly grey hair. I can see in this photo that she was quite small and round, but in my child's eye she was a big woman. She had a powerful personality and was the dominant person in our extended family. Here she is standing, holding me as a baby against her chest. Her beautiful smile shows her warmth and her love for me.

The other photo is of me at five years old with my little brother, Alvin, who was two at the time. We're sitting on the steps of that same house on East 91st Street in Brooklyn. My arm is around him and we're both grinning, happy to be there.

This is the first home I remember. We lived in my grandma's basement when my parents moved back to Brooklyn just after I was born. A Catholic hospital in Reno, Nevada, was an odd place for a Jewish girl of my generation to make her debut in the world. I can't imagine how my mother, Ruth, must have felt, living on the other side of the country from her family. A devoted wife, she had gone west to be with my father, a soldier who was stationed at a base in Nevada during the Second World War. I was born on August 15, 1945, the day Japan announced its surrender, thus ending the war.

My mother's family came to the United States in the late nineteenth century from Russia. My grandfather Harry Schutter immigrated first, to establish a life before bringing his wife and son. My mother was born into a modest but comfortable middle-class home in a Jewish neighbourhood in Brooklyn. She was the middle of three sisters; Ceil, my mother, Ruth, and Clara were close until their deaths. They had an older brother, but he moved to Florida before I was born.

There is no question that Grandma was the matriarch of the family. My grandpa was quiet and kept mostly to himself, but Grandma was a powerful figure in my childhood. Despite the picture I have of her standing in front of the house, holding me as a baby, for as long as I can remember she was always in a wheelchair. As a child I was sure she became crippled falling down the stairs holding me. So I always helped her do the dishes, bake, and cook. I also helped her practise walking with her walker.

Aunt Ceil was the disciplinarian in the family. She was small and mighty and married to Uncle Sol. They had two children, my cousins Bobby and Ann. Aunt Clara was the single aunt and our favourite. She had married twice and gotten annulments rather quickly after both marriages. This was a constant cause of speculation among the adults that we kids never understood and a source of amusement for my father and Uncle Sol that we didn't share. We loved Aunt Clara because she was more fun than Aunt Ceil and she let us stay up late when she babysat.

The only one in her family to graduate from university, my mother was an accountant, a rare profession for a Jewish woman of her generation. When I think of it now, I realize that my mother must have been very strong-minded to have insisted on going to college and getting a degree. She was very intelligent and loved reading; there were always books in the house. Even her older brother didn't get past high school. But after she married my father, she stayed home to raise the kids.

Ruth was quite talented. She did a lot of knitting, needlepoint, and petit point. She was also kind and generous with her niece and nephews, her siblings, and her neighbours.

My strongest memories of Grandma's house were of Passover Seders, a Jewish holiday celebrating Moses' freeing the Jews from slavery in Egypt. Grandma supervised the making of the Seder feast for the whole extended family, and I helped bake the sponge and honey cakes, which we laid out on my grandparents' double bed to cool.

Grandpa would give us a little sweet red wine diluted in seltzer so that we could participate in all the rituals, including dipping our pinkies into the wine for each of the plagues God brought down on the Egyptians. We kids had to fight hilarity during this solemn ceremony, as we had already had enough wine to make us all a little tipsy. My job was to open the door for Elijahu, who represented the stranger we should always invite to the Passover Seder. Opening the door to an invisible being who supposedly drank the glass of red wine in the centre of the table was pretty funny, too. Grandpa tolerated our giggles. It was probably the only way we kids could sit through the endless Passover ceremony.

Until I was almost ten, I lived among grandparents, aunts, uncles, and cousins who were as close to me as my own parents and brothers. My older brother, Leonard (whom we called Lenny at the time), says that our mother's large, warm, extended family was the stability in our lives, the keel that stopped us from overturning in the years that followed.

THE FAMILY OF MY FATHER, Jack, were refugees fleeing the vicious anti-Jewish Russian pogroms that killed two thousand Jews. They made it to Canada in 1916. My father was a toddler when he, his older brother, Norman, and his parents walked across the European continent to a port where they could find safe passage to the new country. Three more children were born later in Canada.

By the time the Rebicks landed in Toronto, the Schutters were already well settled in Brooklyn. Unlike the Schutters, who were among the almost two million Jews in the New York area, the Rebicks found that anti-Semitism was rampant in early-twentieth-century Toronto. The beaches had signs saying, NO DOGS OR JEWS ALLOWED, and my father told stories of having to fight his way to school almost every day against goyish brutes. No doubt he and Norman gave as good as they got, probably better. They had grown up with a violent father who used both humiliation and his fists to discipline his two oldest sons: at seven years old, little Jack was punished by being forced to stand in his father's store window with his pants down. When my father was fifteen he and Norman, both now old enough to fight back, were forcibly shipped off to stay with an aunt in Brooklyn. There, according to one of my father's favourite stories, he fell in with gangsters who loved jazz, booze, reefers, and women, and not necessarily in that order.

As he neared thirty, his doctor told him that if he kept up his lifestyle he wouldn't last long. When he met my mother, a nice middle-class Jewish girl from Brooklyn in her late twenties, he snapped her up. Despite his lack of education, sharp tongue, and sometimes crude behaviour, my mother figured she had quite a catch. When Jack Rebick walked into a room everyone turned to stare. He had a presence, an energy, a kind of charisma. He was a good dancer and an accomplished athlete who looked a little like Gregory Peck. He was tall, and handsome, and luckily, he also turned out to be quite a good provider. In those days, that was all that mattered.

Jack was a great baseball player, a slugger. When he connected with the ball, he almost always hit it out of the park. He was so good that when he joined the army, his base commander in Reno lost the paperwork every time my father was ordered to go overseas so he could stay and entertain the town and the troops there. Later, he was offered a position on the Brooklyn Dodgers farm team, but he turned it down because in those days playing baseball didn't pay enough to raise a family.

Lenny and I loved to watch him play ball, most of the time. Saturday we would watch the Brooklyn Dodgers at Ebbets Field and Sunday we would watch my father play ball. It seemed to us that he was just as good as the pro baseball players. When his ball sailed over the bleachers, he would jog around the bases, half-dancing and wearing a big smile. He could set a dislocated shoulder on the field, too, and that made him seem like a hero to us.

Watching him play baseball was also sometimes a trial. My father was one of the few people who got into fights on the baseball diamond. He'd accuse someone of tripping him and they'd be into it. Sometimes there was just pushing and shoving, but once in a while Jack took a swing. Lenny and I would close our eyes tight, move closer together, and even hold hands, hoping he wouldn't get hurt. Sometimes he'd see us like that, stand up extra tall and strong, and laugh. "Take it easy, nobody's gonna hurt me."

Even after he became a husband and father, Jack kept drinking and sometimes seeing other women, but now he was part of a good family. He thought that would keep him safe, and he was right. My mother took care of him until the day he died, an old man.

MY MEMORY OF THE BASEMENT where we lived until I was five is shadowy and fearful. My older brother, Lenny, and I shared a tiny room under the stairs. My parents' bedroom was on the other side of the wall. There was a living room in the front and a small kitchen. It was dark. I didn't like it there. The only shower was in the corner of Lenny's and my room. Everyone except my father bathed upstairs at my grandma's house. He would come into our room at 4 or 5 a.m. to shower. In most families it's the kids who wake the parents up. Not in ours.

When I was five years old, we moved to East 94th Street, not far from Grandma but too far for us to walk there. We moved into a small three-bedroom modern duplex on the ground floor. I slept in the bedroom off the kitchen. Lenny and Alvin slept on the other side of the house next to my parents' bedroom. I was always scared in that room.

Most people I know who grew up in the 1950s remember their mother best. Not me. I must have spent a lot of time with her — she was home all day — but I remember very little. My father dominated my life.

He was never physically violent with us, but he had an explosive temper. Because his own father beat him and his mother, he promised himself he would never use violence at home; but he often flew into incredible rages. He rarely shouted at my mother, at least not in front of us, but he got mad at us kids a lot and his outbursts were almost completely unpredictable. At the kitchen table, we would be laughing and telling each other stories when suddenly he would start screaming at Lenny for some minor offence. The worst was when Alvin and I would start giggling, especially when Jack woke up from his nap. He would scream at us to stop, but that just made us giggle more, and the more we giggled, the less capable we were of stopping; the more he yelled, the more hysterical our giggles. It was a slowly intensifying dance of hysteria between the man and his children, anger vs. laughter, rage vs. fear. There were no winners.

My father lost his temper more frequently once we moved. I guess he didn't want to display his anger in front of my grandmother or maybe he was under more financial pressure. Decades later, my mother admitted that my father was "a little crazy" when we lived on East 94th Street.

He hit Lenny once. I remember the incident clearly because it was the only time I ever saw Jack apologize. Lenny did something that set him off, but this time, instead of just hollering, he smacked Lenny, who was probably about ten, across the face. My father was very powerful, and he split Lenny's lip, which started to bleed. I don't remember Lenny crying; he must have been in shock. But my father cried. He fell to his knees, taking Lenny's hands in his. "I am so sorry, so sorry," he said through his tears. "It will never happen again," he promised. "Never, never." And it never did.

Both of my brothers tried to stay out of Jack's way, but my strategy was to provoke him. I found it easier to deal with his anger when I knew it was coming than when it came out of nowhere. An early riser, he would be home from work napping on his chair by the time we got home from school and we had to be quiet. *Why can't he nap in the bedroom?* I thought. *Why does he have to plop himself in the middle of the living room?* It made me so mad that accidentally on purpose I'd trip over his feet. He would wake up in a fury, start yelling at me, and then at the boys.

"Why do you have to do it?" Alvin whimpered, but I wouldn't listen.

When I complained to my mother about my father's angry outbursts, she'd only say, "Don't you know your father by now? Why let it bother you?" She figured we should learn to ignore his temper the way she did. He never hit her or even yelled at her very often, but his sarcasm could be like a blow. She put up with a lot but she didn't see it that way. Mostly she made sure that the marriage worked. In those days, when a marriage failed, it was always the woman's fault. And my mother was determined and not willing to fail. Once in a while she defended us against my father's attacks, but she would always back down when he accused her of choosing her children over him. Just before she died, in November 2005, she told me, "Your father and I had a wonderful relationship." I remained silent.

My mother always treated me and my brothers equally and had the same ambitions for all three of us, hoping we would become doctors or lawyers or teachers. We were all expected to do the same chores. She never taught me domestic skills and that was rare. In the way she treated her children, she was a feminist. But it was the fifties so she wanted me to be a pretty little girl. My hair was very long, usually pinned back with a barrette, and in pictures I was always wearing a dress, Mary Jane shoes, and a bow in my long hair.

I may have dressed like a girl, but I liked doing things with the boys. According to my mother, I got expelled from ballet school at age seven because I refused to dance "like that." I was a tomboy, in the parlance of the day. A talented athlete, I was always the first one picked for the team. And I could more than hold my own in fights with my brothers.

"You're more of a man than your brothers," my father used to say to me, insulting all three of us with that single comment.

We used to go to Coney Island in the summer. I remember one year, when I was about four years old, I got lost on the beach. I had come with my mother, Aunt Ceil, Bobby, Ann, and Lenny. Baby Alvin was probably there, too. I don't know how it happened, but somehow I got separated from the family. I remember walking along a beach and seeing grown-ups' legs, so many legs, and I didn't recognize any of them. I was scared, on the verge of tears, and suddenly there was my cousin Bobby. He was seven years older than me, a big boy, and I loved him more than anything. They must have sent him to look for me. I never remember feeling happier than at that moment of running into his arms and looking into his smiling face. I was safe.

Another summer, our extended family went to a cottage near Yonkers for a week. When we were about six, my best friend Johnny Klein (who was my cousins' cousin) and I ran away and climbed into an open pipe that was sitting on some grass. Our fathers were searching for us but we were hiding. The sad part is that by that time, I didn't really want to be found.

I WAS NINE YEARS OLD when my mother told me that we were moving to Toronto. She sat down on my bed just before bedtime. Lenny was still up in the living room. He was three years older and sometimes got to stay up later.

"Judy, I have something important to talk to you about."

"Okay," I murmured, wondering immediately what I might have done wrong that day. It was rare for my mother to speak with me privately so I figured I was in trouble.

"Daddy and I have decided to move to Toronto this summer. He is going into business with his brothers. You'll love it there, Judy. You have so many cousins and we'll have a big house."

"But I don't know those cousins. I want to stay here with Bobby and Ann and Johnny."

"Daddy has a very good job there. He wants to go. It will be better for all of us," she replied. I knew she didn't want to go. How could she? It was her family we were leaving.

"And what about Grandma? Who'll take care of her if we leave? Tell Daddy we don't want to go. Please."

"Don't worry, dear," she said with her usual calm assurance. "Aunt Ceil and Aunt Clara will take care of Grandma, and we'll visit all the time."

"But our family is here," I insisted. "Why do you want to leave our family? What'll we do without them?" *What would I do without them?* "I'm not going. I'll stay here with Grandma."

"No, you won't." My mother was losing her patience. "Daddy has decided."

"It isn't fair." I didn't cry. I never cried anymore.

But it was the first time I consciously thought about the power my father had over the family.

Four

TORONTO

WE MOVED FROM BROOKLYN to Toronto in July 1955, just before my tenth birthday. Crossing the border was the first time I had ever had to sign something—I think it was the landed card. I felt very grown up and still remember reaching up to the counter to sign my name. But even that didn't change how I felt about the move. I was heartbroken.

My father's parents still lived downtown on Markham Street, and my aunts and uncles lived north of them in Forest Hill. My parents had moved us even farther north, to a suburb called North York, which at the time was still mostly farmland. We lived in a detached bungalow on Waterloo Avenue with a big front lawn and a huge backyard. We didn't even have a backyard in Brooklyn. In Toronto, we had so much space. Jewish families were buying houses in a new subdivision in the suburbs. We were one of the first Jewish families in the neighbourhood. In Brooklyn, I didn't think much about being Jewish—almost everyone we knew was Jewish.

That first fall, I was coming home from Wilmington Elementary School when I saw Lenny surrounded by a group of big farm boys. He was thirteen at the time and still quite small. The boys pushed him down and started pummelling him, calling him names.

"You stink, dirty Jew boy."

"You're yellow like all them Jews, scaredy-cat."

I was shocked. They were *hitting* my brother. I got mad and jumped them. "Leave my brother alone!" I cried, pounding their backs with my little fists.

Laughing, they said, "Hey, Jew boy, your sister's more of a man than you are." An eerie echo of my father.

We told my mother about the taunts, but Lenny made me promise I wouldn't tell her or Daddy what really happened, that I had rescued him from the beating. Always tolerant, she responded, "Don't call them dirty Christian just because they call you dirty Jew." My mother was very careful to make sure we didn't have or express prejudice against others. When my parents could afford house cleaners, they were usually Black women. I remember when Alvin was two or three he was fascinated that our cleaning lady had such dark skin. My mother explained to all of us that different people had different colour skin and sometimes different accents because they came from a different part of the country or a different part of the world. I never remember her putting a higher value on being Jewish, and it's something I've always appreciated about my mother.

Still, it didn't stop me from socking one of my classmates

in the face when she yelled, "Dirty Jew!" at me. No doubt I remembered my father's stories of fighting the goyim in downtown Toronto. After that, no one called me "dirty Jew" again.

Less than a year after we moved to Toronto, my grandmother died. I had never seen my mother cry before. I remember feeling sad, but for some reason I didn't cry. I was convinced she had died because I wasn't there to take care of her. I still think it was possible that she died of a broken heart, losing both my mother and me.

I remember my mother put her arm around me when she told me. It was a rare show of affection. The most I could ever hope for was a peck on the cheek.

"Aren't you sad that Grandma died?" she asked me.

"Yeah, sure."

"You loved her so much. Aren't you sad that she's gone? I am sad and Daddy is sad. What about you?"

"I'm sad, too," I said, but I refused to cry. "Are you mad at me?"

"Why would I be?"

"It's my fault."

"What are you talking about, Judy?"

"I know she died 'cause of me. You don't have to pretend."

"She didn't die because of you. What are you talking about?"

"I know what happened. She fell holding me when I was a baby and that's why she's crippled, and she died 'cause I wasn't there to take care of her."

"Where in the world did you hear that story? It's not true. She got sick and her sickness made her crippled. She had a tumour on her spine. It was when you were a baby but it wasn't because of you. Anyway, she didn't die from the tumour. She died of old age."

I never got to say goodbye to my grandmother or participate in the collective grief of the family. My parents thought that children should not attend funerals, so Lenny, Alvin, and I stayed in Toronto with a babysitter while my parents were in Brooklyn. Whatever grief I might have had for my grandmother was buried along with everything else.

AFTER MY GRANDMA DIED, my dissociation went into overdrive. My memories of my childhood in Toronto are pretty sketchy. I remember school, camp, going to the Jewish Y on Sunday mornings when my father played handball and we went swimming, and I remember going out for dinner either to the Steak Pit on Avenue Road or to China House on Eglinton Avenue.

I do remember that my father changed once we moved to Toronto. He went into the hardwood flooring business with his family and started making a lot of money. If you live in a building that was constructed in the 1960s or 1970s in Toronto, you're probably walking on floors they installed. He became successful and was admired by people around him. Jack made and lost several fortunes in his lifetime but that never bothered him. He was a risk taker and enjoyed living the good life. He gave my mother beautiful jewellery, a lot of it smuggled across the border, and they travelled a lot, especially on cruises. He went on regular junkets to Las Vegas. Jack was a gambler, betting with bookies in Toronto on every sports game going. He didn't worship money, though, and he didn't teach us to feel insecure without it.

Generally, my mother was the parent who taught us how to behave. My father took us out to baseball, dinner, and concerts. He taught us through his behaviour neither to respect authority nor to follow the rules. He broke the law with impunity, had no problem standing up to cops or any other authority. He had episodes of uncontrollable rage, which frightened us, but my mother was more the disciplinarian when that was necessary.

My father wasn't like other people's parents. He was exciting, unpredictable, funny, handsome, charming, and had gangster friends. I still occasionally meet people who have stories about him. So despite the fights, the rage, and the humiliation he caused me, my brothers, and my friends, I loved him.

During the first couple of years we lived in Toronto, we went to Brooklyn a lot. Before the New York State Thruway was finished it was a twelve-hour drive. We three kids sat in the back and spent our time singing Broadway musical tunes. I still remember most of the lyrics to those songs. My parents didn't sing but they enjoyed music: jazz, Louis Armstrong, Frank Sinatra, Ella Fitzgerald, Sarah Vaughan. Some of my happy memories are of those road trips. After my grandfather died in 1960, we didn't go to New York as often. In Toronto, it was the neighbours that became our community. Because my father didn't get along with most of his family, they were not a part of our daily lives. We visited my father's parents and occasionally my aunts and uncles, but my mother's friends were the neighbourhood women she played mah-jong with and my father socialized with his business associates.

I also remember Rusty, our dog. She was a beautiful Irish Setter but not very well behaved. Leonard and I trained Rusty to jump on Alvin; as a result Alvin was afraid of her. My father would hit Rusty with a newspaper when she mis-behaved but that only made her wilder when he wasn't home. One time my mother baked a couple of apple pies, my fath-er's favourite, and left them on the kitchen counter to cool. Before we knew it Rusty had eaten a pie and crushed the other one with her paw. Soon after, Rusty disappeared; my father gave her away. I don't remember how long we had her or whether my mother agreed with the decision, all I know is that we blamed Daddy. Everything bad was always his fault.

While things continued to be volatile at home, school was a different story. Grade six was my best year. Alvin remem-bers that year I came into my own, telling stories about school at the dinner table and generally taking up more space. I do remember gaining more confidence in myself that year. I especially remember Mr. Subden. He not only recog-nized my talents, but he also helped me overcome my fears. I was afraid of tumbling, standing on my head, or doing a somersault during gym class. He didn't order me to do it or excuse me from doing it. He helped me overcome my fear by supporting me. His kindness was like a calming balm. I even invited him home for dinner. I also remember my grade seven teacher, the towering, authoritative Miss Martin who wasn't married and seemed very happy.

After this I remember almost nothing about school. The years between grade eight and eleven are missing from my memory. I suppose it's not an accident that this would have been about the time when I was moving into puberty. But a few key incidents stick out in my mind.

When I turned fourteen, I went on my first real date. Marty Silverstein, one of the most popular boys at camp, asked me out on New Year's Eve. I was beyond thrilled. I don't remember either of my parents objecting to the date beforehand; no doubt if they had I wouldn't have gone out with him.

When Marty arrived at my house to pick me up, my father came to the door.

"Hello, young man?"

"Hello, sir," Marty replied nervously.

"I hope you know that I expect you to take care of my daughter and get her home on time."

"Sure thing," Marty answered.

Anxious to get out as quickly as possible, I started to put my boots on.

"What's wrong with you, young man?" my father said in a raised voice.

"What do you mean, sir?"

"Didn't your parents teach you any manners?" Jack was now booming.

Marty was confused and frightened.

"Help her put on her boots, for Christ's sake," my father bellowed, moving in to grab Marty's shoulders and force him to the ground.

"Stop it, Daddy. I can put on my own boots," I insisted, but it just made him angrier.

Marty quickly got down on his hands and knees to help

me. He was humiliated and I was angry. Marty was the perfect date: Jewish, handsome, from a well-to-do family, a good student. If my father wouldn't even accept Marty, what was the point? As long as I was living at home, I would never go on another date.

When I look back, it seems very extreme that I would give up on dating after that incident, especially since I stood up to my father on other issues. Now I think that his reaction to my dating was more threatening to my subconscious mind and I probably dissociated from my sexual feelings entirely until I was much older. I did once make out with a boy at camp when I was sixteen, but we got caught and I was lectured by the camp director, which no doubt reinforced the unfelt fear.

Another memory that has stayed with me was when I experienced my first anxiety attack at camp at age fifteen. I felt a tightness and fluttering in my chest and went for a walk in the woods to get away from the girls in my cabin. My counsellor noticed I was missing and came looking for me. I didn't know why I was feeling so anxious and I don't remember what she did to calm me down.

A year later, I suffered a clinical depression. I had just had my sweet sixteen party, a wonderful, elaborate event. There were printed invitations, the dress was semi-formal, and everyone was assigned a date. My father even had a dance floor built in the backyard. It was a lovely celebration, and I was pretty, popular, and a good student—all the things that were supposed to make you happy. But for some reason it made me feel desperately alone.

During this time, my father was away a lot. His conflict

with his father and his brother Irving, who ran their hardwood flooring business, was getting worse. Jack decided a business to manufacture flooring would be a good addition to their operation and the others agreed. He started going to Montreal to explore the possibilities and decided to open a factory in Sherbrooke, Quebec.

A phone call that year made me question why he was away so much. My mother was down the street playing mahjong and we kids were alone at home. The phone rang and Lenny answered it.

"I want to talk to your father," a man said angrily.

"Sorry, my father's not here," he responded politely.

"I know he's not there," the man yelled. "He's in a hotel fucking my wife. Tell him that I'm going down there to kill him."

We huddled together trying to decide what to do. *Should we call the police? What will we say? If we call the police, Mom will find out. Daddy can take care of himself but maybe we should warn him. We don't know where he is. What are we gonna do?*

We didn't do anything. Jack called that night from Montreal. He was fine. We were relieved. We weren't really surprised that Jack was cheating. He had already bragged to Lenny that he had slept with another woman the day after his wedding. So we figured he was still cheating on my mother. But this call made it more dangerous.

That winter, I had an undiagnosed illness that kept me in bed for more than a month. There were no real symptoms, just extreme fatigue and a lack of interest in anything. My marks in school went down 30 percent. The doctor

47

diagnosed a virus because he had no idea what was wrong. I realize now that it was my first clinical depression. Many years later, I met my pediatrician Dr. Gerry Cohen and his wife, Dr. May Cohen, both of whom were important medical leaders in the pro-choice movement. I asked Gerry if he remembered me as a teenager and this particular illness. He did and agreed it could very well have been a depression, since little was known about teenage depression back then.

After the depression, I gained a lot of weight, about forty pounds by the time I was eighteen. I was so skinny as a child that my mother had to buy suspenders to keep my skirt up. I started gaining weight once I hit puberty. At fourteen I weighed 125 pounds, 136 at fifteen, 148 at sixteen. By the time I was eighteen I weighed 180 pounds.

Eating was comforting and being bigger than other girls made me feel safe. Being overweight also meant that boys weren't as interested in me, so I didn't have to work very hard to avoid going out with them, knowing that my father would make my life miserable if I did. Maybe I was looking to create a reason for my unhappiness that I could understand.

Five

"IT WAS McGILL THAT RUINED YOU"

IN 1962, MY FATHER decided we would move to Montreal. The planned move gave me something to look forward to. I had friends and was active in the student council in high school, but still I was miserable. I was sure university would be much more stimulating and I would have more independence.

My father had an architect friend of his design our new home. It was a two-storey ranch-style house with a floating staircase in front of a huge picture window. From the outside it looked like a mansion. There were four bedrooms, a large living room, dining room, kitchen, and den.

My strongest memory of that house was running up the stairs after a fight with my father and slamming the door to my bedroom, where I was spending more and more time alone. My strategy to avoid fighting with my father was to invite my friends over, in the vain hope that Jack might behave himself or at the very least have a new target to occupy him. The first time my friend Susan Swan came over, he attacked her for not accepting the offer of seconds of what was certainly roast beef, mashed potatoes, and peas and carrots after a hearty soup and a chicken liver *forshpeis* (appetizer) — our usual Sabbath dinner.

"What's the matter, don't like our kike food?" he berated her.

Susan, who had never met a Jew before going to McGill, was horrified and looked to me for rescue. All I could do was roll my eyes. She had seconds and thirds, but that just encouraged him. I had warned her about Jack — we always warned our friends about my father's "sense of humour." He was almost always mean and could be very cruel. Susan never came back.

I can still hear my mother's voice: "It's just your father, Judy. Don't you know him by now? Why do you get so upset?" "Grin and bear it" was her motto, though I believe his behaviour never really bothered her.

MY ACTIVISM BEGAN the day I walked into the *McGill Daily* office in downtown Montreal in the fall of 1964. The office occupied most of the basement of the old Student Union building. At the centre of the office was a semicircular desk where the editors sat each day. There were a couple of offices along the wall for the editor and managing editor; the rest of us sat in a large open room at whatever desk was empty. The room functioned as a social space as well as a workspace.

The *Daily* was the centre of radicalism at McGill. The New Left, which was what we called the radical student movement in the United States and Britain, had been redefining left-wing politics for a couple of years, mostly on campus. The New Left rejected the old leftist ideas of social democracy and Communism. The focus was on democracy and fulfilling the promise of government for, by, and of the people. I didn't know anything about political activism but I loved the energy, the excitement, and the people involved in the movement. They were like me: misfits. Instead of admitting ignorance, I just kept my mouth shut, listened, worked hard, and dressed all in black so I looked like a radical. Everyone thought I was a lot savvier than I was.

My first byline was for an article covering a speech given by pioneer feminist Laura Sabia to the McGill Women's Union in November 1964. Mrs. Sabia was appealing to the "girls," as we would have been called then, to stay in school. "The natural instinct to have children will be just as strong when you are thirty as it is when you are twenty," she explained.

Women were first admitted to McGill in 1884 but were not allowed to join the Students' Society until 1931. The Women's Union at McGill was founded during the First World War to organize care packages for soldiers; thereafter it continued to give women students a voice. In the 1960s, things were beginning to change. In 1964 Joy Fenston was the editor of the *Daily*, and the following year Sharon Sholzberg was the first female president of the Students' Society. It would be a few years before the new generation of feminists, no doubt some of them in that very room, began their revolution. Looking at old issues of the *Daily*, it is clear that I had what we probably called the women's beat.

At the *Daily*, I met girls who seemed like they didn't quite fit in, like me: Susan Swan, a tall magnificent creature who with her upper-class WASP background was no less exotic to me than if she had been from outer space. She was the only girl at McGill to ever quit a rushing for a sorority, but she still looked like a sorority girl. She felt out of place at the *Daily*, which was full of mostly bohemian Jewish radicals, but she loved writing. I befriended her because she seemed so different and because I secretly wanted to be a writer, too. The beatnik look that I affected fooled her into thinking I belonged there so she was grateful for my friendship. And a great friendship it became, lasting until today. Honey Dresher was, like me, a nice Jewish girl who didn't accept the future laid out before her. We quickly became friends and had a wonderful time together. And then there was editor Joy Fenston. Tough and serious, Joy was like no other girl I'd ever met. We never became friends but she was an inspiration. I don't think Joy took any particular interest in promoting female writers, but her presence was inspiration enough.

I remember the excitement of my first demonstration that fall. It was the year that three civil rights workers who had travelled south to assist with voter registration for Blacks were murdered in Mississippi. We marched to protest the minimal sentences given to the perpetrators.

The *Daily* gave me the opportunity to stay away from home, too. We worked long hours and when we were "on the desk," those hours stretched until after midnight. It

drove my father mad. I assume he didn't like my growing independence, and Lenny was away at school so Jack
didn't have him to pick on. That left only Alvin, and Jack
almost never picked on Alvin. The difference between me
and Lenny was that I fought back.

"It was McGill that ruined you," he would say for years
after.

1965 WAS THE YEAR that changed everything. Patrick
MacFadden became the editor of the *Daily*. He was Irish,
quite a bit older than the rest of us being in his late twenties,
married with children, well schooled in the radical politics
and culture of the time, and a consummate womanizer.
Most of us were in our late teens, enamoured by the growing
youth movement in the United States and a little awestruck
by his greater knowledge and charisma. We hung on his
every word.

At the first meeting that term, Patrick said, "We're going
to change what the *Daily* is."

Patrick made good on that promise, transforming the
Daily from an ordinary campus newspaper focused on student politics, sports, fraternities, and events to the centre of
radical activism at McGill. What that meant in 1965 was
challenging the administration and the right-wing elements
on campus, particularly those on the student council. It also
meant supporting the civil rights movement and national
liberation struggles around the world, including the one in
Quebec, and of course opposing the war in Vietnam. This
was the period when the Front de libération du Québec

(FLQ) was calling for a socialist insurrection and the overthrow of the Quebec government. The independence movement in Quebec was modelled on many of the anticolonial liberation struggles. McGill University, a central Anglo institution, was a major target of their attacks.

After Patrick wrote a particularly nasty editorial criticizing right-wing student leaders, there was a campaign to fire him as editor of the *Daily* on the grounds that he did not represent the students. The charge against him was "consistent use of the *Daily* for extreme political purposes" and "lack of coverage of traditional student activities."

Patrick responded, "It is the job of the *Daily* to speak *to* students, not to speak *for* them."

He was fired. Some of the radicals on council held an open meeting for students, who almost unanimously opposed the decision. Patrick was reinstated within two days. I learned a lot from him, including how to stand up to attack.

Patrick's reinstatement was the first sign that the majority of the students were on our side against the conservative forces at McGill that had dominated the campus for years. In the early and mid-sixties the student council resisted the changes that were sweeping North America. The *Daily* represented the new forces of change, so we were often at loggerheads.

It was also in 1965 that the anti-war movement took off. I went to a demonstration protesting the war in Vietnam sponsored by the Quebec student union, UGEQ. More than four thousand students showed up. In the past, activism at McGill had consisted of a small cabal of radicals at the

Daily. Now McGill erupted with activism, as did many other campuses across Quebec and Canada. Student Union for Peace Action (SUPA) emerged from a national conference in Saskatchewan in 1965 and went on to lead the anti-war movement for the next couple of years.

Free love was the prevailing ideology on the *Daily.* While I doubt anyone but Patrick practised it, we all thought we should be completely free about our sexuality. That fall they showed a pornographic film at a party in the *Daily* office. I had never seen such a film and found it deeply disturbing. I didn't say anything for fear of seeming like I wasn't hip, but I was really upset. I left and so did a couple of other women. The objection was likely more about how inappropriate it was to show the film in mixed company rather than to show it at all. A lot of the guys thought it was a problem, too, especially once the women left, so it never happened again.

By that time, Patrick was pressuring me to sleep with him. But I had a problem. I was still a virgin. While radicals and bohemians were promoting free love, the mores of the 1950s were still with us. Single women couldn't get birth control and most men wouldn't use a condom. I was embarrassed to be a virgin, so I pretended I wasn't.

In Canada disseminating information about birth control was still illegal. The famous *McGill Birth Control Handbook*, published in 1968, was the first information any of us had about birth control from a female perspective. Our ignorance about sex was monumental. Perhaps some of us had read *Lady Chatterley's Lover*, or if we were really bold Henry Miller's *Tropic of Cancer*, but these were descriptions of sex from a decidedly masculine perspective.

For me, Patrick was the perfect solution. He was easy about sex, interested, and available. I told him I was a virgin and asked him to promise not to tell anyone. We did it in the tiny dorm-like room he had as editor in the McGill Student Union. It didn't hurt that much but there was a lot of blood, and he just stuffed the sheets in the cupboard. Afterward he asked me if I had had an orgasm. When I said I hadn't, he suggested something might be wrong with me. Patrick did me the favour of taking my virginity, but he also gave me a complex about my sexuality. I worried that maybe I was frigid, in the language of the time.

Then one of the *Daily* staffers found the sheets.

"Jesus, Judy, you were a virgin and you slept with Patrick?" he said with a look of what I took to be pity but was probably real concern. I denied it. Everyone knew that I had slept with Patrick and everyone knew that Patrick had sex with every woman he could. The guys thought he was a real ass to have seduced me, since sex was so meaningless to him.

"No, I am not a virgin," I answered. "I just have a problem that means I sometimes bleed when I have sex." I hated being treated like a girl, someone to be protected and sheltered. So I lied. I doubt anyone believed me, but they stopped treating me that way.

While I was ignorant about sex, I did know that birth control was important. I knew too many girls whose life or health was ruined by having a baby when they weren't ready or having a backstreet abortion out of desperation. Why should a woman pay the price of an unwanted pregnancy? In those days it was rare for a man to take responsibility for getting a girl pregnant. When a friend asked if I knew about

56

how to get in touch with a doctor in town that was doing abortions, I made it my business to find out and became part of an underground network referring women to safe illegal abortions.

This was also the year I started smoking. Pretty well everyone smoked cigarettes in those days but because both of my parents smoked, I didn't. Whatever they did, I didn't want to do. But I was often nervous. I'd be sitting with a crowd of *Daily* staffers drinking beer and peeling the labels off the bottles. Someone would say, "For Christ's sake, Judy, take a cigarette and cut that out." The Surgeon General's report linking smoking and lung cancer came out in early 1964, but no one took it seriously. I resisted for a while but then one fateful day, I took the offered cigarette. At first it made me sick but I kept trying. Within a couple of years I was chain-smoking. I've since learned through my own attempts to quit that in addition to being powerfully addictive, cigarettes are a drug that help keep your feelings down. And during this time in my life I was powerfully emotional in ways that came dangerously close to exposing my hidden memories.

Six

LOVE LOST

OVER THE SUMMER OF 1965, a lot changed in my household, too. My father's business went bankrupt. He blamed his younger brother Frank, who he had brought in to manage the place.

"Frank turned that place into a shit factory." He would pause for effect. "Frank has always had a talent for turning money into shit," ending with a wry smile. And Frank was his favourite brother. He had been anxious to put some distance between himself and the rest of his family but that attempt had failed. I think it was probably his gambling that actually wrecked the business. He seemed to always be in court. But nothing was ever my father's fault. Both he and my mother always put the blame elsewhere.

I don't know what his connections were to the Montreal mob, which was deeply involved in the construction industry, but he was good friends with Johnny Sacco, a famous gangster from Buffalo who a couple of decades later became an informant for the FBI. My father's amicable relationship with him must have meant he was much more involved with the mob than I realized, though not enough to save his business.

One Friday night during my second year at McGill, Johnny Sacco brought his girlfriend to our house. She looked very much the part of a gangster's moll, which is exactly what she was. She was loud, funny, a little racy, and had a cleavage that seemed to jump out at you. We loved her but my mother was not so enthusiastic. My father's escapades could be amusing and that night he was in great form. Sacco loved him and entertained us all. A couple of weeks later, we saw him being led away in handcuffs on Buffalo TV news.

"Don't worry," my father said. "He always gets out." My mother was not amused.

The bankruptcy meant my parents would be moving back to Toronto, and I would stay in Montreal to finish my studies at McGill. Alvin, who was still in high school, went to Toronto before my parents in time for the beginning of the school year. For the same reason I moved out before school started. Leonard and his new wife, Maureen O'Donnell, also moved to Toronto to their own apartment. It was the first time I'd be living apart from my family.

I moved into a Park Avenue studio at the end of August 1966, and in October I met a man named Roger. I was at a house party on Milton Avenue with some friends, when this older guy started talking to me. He had a handlebar moustache and a bit of a beer belly, and he was very British. His eyes crinkled up when he smiled, making him look like the kindest person you might ever meet. Roger was, to say the least, persistent. He came back to my apartment with me, even though I wasn't really sure I wanted to go to bed with him. We made love that night.

At thirty-four Roger was a renaissance man who read a book a day and remembered everything he read. He could talk intelligently about almost any subject, although he was obsessed with some. He made me feel beautiful, smart, and desirable. He also introduced me to sex and drugs. I had tried both before, but Roger was the full-spectrum experience.

Roger loved women—all women. When he was drinking, he would hit on and have sex with almost every woman he met if she was willing. We had sex several times a day, whether or not he was sleeping with other women. I had an inkling that this was unusual behaviour, but it took a few years before I realized how hypersexual he really was. He said it was fine for me to sleep with others, too, although he always found a reason why one guy or another was no good for me.

Once Roger moved in, my apartment on Park Avenue became a social centre. He was plugged into Montreal's bohemian scene: artists, writers, poets, and drug dealers. Even in those exotic circles, Roger stood out as the one willing to break all the rules. For my friends, just coming out of their teenage years, Roger and his friends were spellbinding.

My friends loved Roger almost as much as I did. He was more than ten years older than most of us and had a million stories. But more than that, he was kind and caring. One of my friends who hung out with us a lot was Bob Chodos. He was smart and a great writer but very insecure socially. He used a cane, which drew attention to his disability. Roger, in his usual direct fashion, told Bob he was certain he could walk without it. Then he took it away and challenged Bob to walk. From that day on, Bob walked without his cane. Roger was like that: he gave you confidence that you didn't know you had.

Roger believed in absolute honesty in relationships — or so he said. It pained him that I was lying to my parents about being with him. I knew my father would go crazy if he ever met Roger, but Roger wouldn't let up about meeting my parents. Then one weekend my parents decided to go to Toronto to get ready for the move. Roger insisted that I show him my house in Côte-Saint-Luc.

When Roger saw the house he said, "You told me your father was a businessman, but you didn't say you lived in a mansion."

"It's not really a mansion," I replied. "It looks bigger than it is."

Within a few minutes, Roger got into my father's liquor cabinet. After a few drinks, he decided to put on a yarmulke and take off everything else. He sat rabbi-like, in his mind, at the dining-room table, facing the picture window. He started making a speech about the military brilliance of the Israeli army generals, his current obsession. It was just after the Six-Day War, in which Israel had captured the Gaza Strip from Egypt, the West Bank from Jordan, and the Golan Heights from Syria. My obsession was to get him to stop drinking and get dressed.

To allay my anxiety, I called the hotel where my parents

were staying to make sure they weren't coming back early. Sure enough, they were on their way home. I phoned Sam, Roger's boss at the motel where he worked as a designer. In those days drive-in movies were illegal in Quebec. Roger had the idea of designing a geodesic dome to house a movie theatre at this motel, which was a hangout for artists and druggies just outside of Montreal. I asked Sam to come and pick up Roger. All the while I was begging Roger to get dressed.

He put on his clothes just before my parents walked in the door. I went to greet them and tried to introduce Roger from a distance so they wouldn't notice how drunk he was. Detecting my father's rising anger, my mother suggested some coffee and cake. We stood in the kitchen, my father with his back to the refrigerator, my mother busying herself making coffee, and me standing between the two men, trying to keep Roger at some kind of distance from Jack.

It didn't take long for the storm of my father's anger to break.

"Get that man out of my house!" he shouted.

I quietly tried to talk Roger into waiting outside the front door. Roger puffed out his chest, walked military-style around me, marched up to my father, and said, "Sir, are you aware of the brilliance of the Israeli generals?"

"What the hell are you talking about?" Jack replied.

"They learned those manoeuvres from British generals," Roger continued. "There is an important alliance between the Jews and the British, sir."

I feared what was coming next.

"Let's all just calm down," my mother said with a familiar

look of dismay. "I'm sure we can work this out. Would you like to stay for dinner?"

"Are you out of your goddamn mind?" my father thundered. "I don't want him here another minute!"

Just then the doorbell rang. "Please, Roger," I said, dragging him by the arm. "Sam is here to pick you up. Please come with me."

"I'm going to take you away from this terrible man," Roger said as I pushed him out the door. Finally rid of him, I slumped against the door, his words reverberating in my mind, running up against his actions.

"If you keep seeing that man, you are no longer my daughter!" my father shouted from the kitchen. Predictably, the storm was turning against me now. As much as I hated to admit it, I could see his point. Roger was great, but I had never seen him so drunk and out of control. My family was still important to me and I didn't doubt my father's threat.

"Okay," I said, "I won't see him anymore." That didn't stop the tide of invective. By the end of it my father was satisfied that I was not going to see "that man" again.

I told Roger that I just couldn't handle this kind of confrontation with my father and it would be better to end the relationship. What I didn't say was that maybe I couldn't handle him either. I don't remember what he said in response, but he kept coming over, and after a week or so we were back together again.

A few weeks later my parents moved to Toronto.

THE WINTER GOT more and more intense. I became entrenched in Roger's bohemian lifestyle. In addition to the non-stop visitors, we were doing a lot of drugs. LSD had been flowing into Montreal for about a year. Roger and I had taken it a couple of times with a friend who acted as our guide. An acid trip was considered a spiritual experience and the drug was very strong, so it was a good idea to do it with someone who could help you through it.

In February 1967, in my tiny Park Avenue apartment, we dropped what turned out to be very strong LSD with my friends Alan and Diane, whom I had met that summer in an amateur theatre group. It was the middle of a snowstorm so we were planning on staying indoors. Acid comes on slowly. It takes about an hour before your perception of the world is completely transformed. I'd taken it a couple of times before and mostly saw pretty moving colours. Solid objects turned into viscous liquids and sometimes I felt like I was floating in space. But this time was different. Suddenly I was looking up at everyone. I had turned into a child. The closer I got to Roger, the smaller I got. When I was next to him, I felt as if I were five years old.

Panic set in. At first I went into the bathroom to look at myself in the mirror. If I could see myself in the mirror, I couldn't have turned into a child. The face looking back at me was distorted, but it was me. My heart slowed a bit and I walked back into the living room. As soon as I saw Roger I became a child again. I had to get out of there. Panicked, I decided the best route was the fire escape. Roger would follow me down the stairs, but not onto the fire escape. We were five floors up.

"Stop!" Alan yelled. "Judy, stop."

But I didn't. I opened the door. Alan grabbed my arm.

"I have to get out of here," I cried. Alan looked at Roger for help.

"Keep him away from me," I cried. "I can't be near him."

"It's okay, Judy," Roger said in his warm, loving voice. "I won't hurt you. It's me, Roger. You know me. We'll go outside but let's go down the stairs. It's safer."

"You go first, then," I said, not wanting to risk being near him.

Alan helped me down the stairs and onto the street. Once we were outside, I became myself again.

I was deeply disturbed by this experience. At the time I didn't understand I was experiencing some form of dissociation or a split into another personality, but I did sense my psyche was showing me something that I didn't want to see. Unwilling to look inward, I looked at how I was living. Roger was getting harder to handle. I was working less and less on the *Daily* and not going to school at all. Once I came down from the trip, I knew we had to talk.

"I felt like a little girl around you," I explained. "I couldn't be myself when I was near you. I don't know what to do. I love being with you but I have to live my own life and I feel like being with you is stopping me from doing that."

"I want you to live your own life, too," he replied lovingly. "I don't want you to be my wife. It's because you are so strong and independent that I love you. I don't want you to change. I want you to be your own person."

That was the last time I took LSD. I liked being high but I couldn't stand losing control. Something stopped me from going further down this self-destructive path. It might have been Simon, the guardian personality, but of course I knew nothing about that at the time.

THERE WAS NO way that Roger and I could continue living in that tiny apartment so we decided to find a bigger place with Alan and Diane. We found a wonderful old Victorian house on Hutchison Street, a couple of blocks from my apartment.

We moved in on May 1, 1967. I paid our portion of the rent because Roger didn't have a job; he just did the odd contract here and there. I have never understood why Alan and Diane agreed to live with us, given Roger's drinking and mercurial ways. But like most of my friends, they found Roger fascinating and we were all very close friends. I guess for the three of us, moving in together was another step into the sixties lifestyle. Living together without marriage was radical enough in 1967, but sharing a house with another couple was almost like living in a San Francisco commune.

Roger started drinking more once we moved to Hutchison Street. His womanizing, which hadn't bothered me until then, got much worse. When he was drunk, he lost all impulse control and would come on to women right in front of me. He would also crash dinner parties and disrupt the proceedings. The worst was when he would pick up people on the street or in a bar and bring them home. These parties would inevitably erupt into loud, boisterous, and sometimes threatening scenes.

One night when I was visiting my parents in Toronto, Alan

and Diane hosted a reception for friends who had just gotten married. Roger crashed the party with some of his "friends." That was the incident that put Alan over the edge. They got into a physical confrontation and Alan knocked a dead-drunk Roger to the ground. Like many drunks, Roger never remembered or took responsibility for his behaviour. The next day he felt that Alan had done him an injustice and tried to have him criminally charged for assault. That was it for Alan. He and Diane decided to leave. They asked me to come with them but I wasn't ready to give up on the relationship yet.

"We couldn't understand it," Alan told me many years later. "Things were really coming unglued for you, too. It was the only time in my life I was completely paralyzed. Roger was getting incredible — intolerant, mean, crazy. You were just like a zombie, more or less. You totally zoned out. Roger being extremely crazy, you being zoned out, and we being unable to cope — we couldn't survive. We thought you should come with us but you wouldn't come."

I blocked out the whole experience. It wasn't until I tracked down Alan in preparing this memoir that he told me the story. I had confirmation of my dissociation in the past from someone else. While he was talking I had a flashback in black and white of me standing in the hallway of the Hutchison house looking into the living room, seeing and feeling nothing. Before that moment, it had always been a mystery to me why Alan and Diane moved out. I just knew that they did and I never saw them after that. I often wonder why I never tried to find out why Alan and Diane left. Perhaps part of my conscious mind was telling me to leave well enough alone.

ALAN AND DIANE's departure made Roger dry out for a while. For one thing we couldn't really afford the house ourselves so he had to find work. He also probably realized that his behaviour would eventually drive me out as well.

Still, he was always inviting people to crash at our place. Usually I was the one who objected to total strangers staying with us, but in early August our roles were suddenly reversed. The doorbell rang at 11 a.m. and standing there was a hippie. Roger and his friends didn't think much of hippies. They brought too much attention to the LSD that had been flooding into Montreal, restricting their freedom to partake whenever the spirit moved them. But this guy was all business.

"Hi, my name is Larry. I'm the road manager for Jefferson Airplane and the Grateful Dead," he said. "Paul Krassner told us about Roger and he sounded cool. We'd like to crash at your place for a couple of days while we're here for Expo."

Jefferson Airplane was just about the biggest rock band around, but I had never heard of the Grateful Dead.

"How many people?" I asked.

"About twenty with our old ladies and groupies," he said. "But we don't all need beds. It's cool to crash on couches and the floor."

I went upstairs to try to rouse Roger but he was dead to the world. So I said yes because Roger always welcomed guests. A couple of hours later when the bus pulled up, Roger was out the back door. He didn't want to deal with the chaos and he didn't care a whit about celebrities. One time when Rudolf Nureyev, the famed Russian dancer, was in Montreal, a friend came to our table at the famous

Spanish Club saying breathlessly, "Nureyev is here; he's right there."

"Is he dancing?" Roger asked dryly. If not, he wasn't interested.

But I was excited that Haight-Ashbury had come to my house in Montreal. It is almost impossible to understand today the ethic that made a hugely successful rock 'n' roll band crash on the floor of someone's house, but that was the 1960s. Only Jefferson Airplane's Grace Slick stayed at a hotel.

"She always does," one of the band members said contemptuously.

All of them except Pigpen of the Grateful Dead, who was a drinker, seemed stoned all the time, not just on pot but on acid. Even though I didn't know anything about the Dead, I found them the most interesting. Jerry Garcia always had a guitar slung around his neck. He never stopped practising. His "old lady," in the parlance of the day, was Mountain Girl, and they had a baby named Sunrise. Garcia was the philosopher of the group, and he and Pigpen would often have long discussions. I remember sitting around the kitchen table, Garcia and Mountain Girl doing most of the talking. Mountain Girl, who I later found out was one of the Merry Pranksters, was probably the most stoned-out person I had ever met.

"I'd love to go to China," she said in the kitchen apropos of nothing I could see. "Imagine, everyone's Chinese."

"Cool," everyone responded.

They were great guests. They brought in all kinds of good food and they cleaned the house from top to bottom when they left. I guess it was part of the communal lifestyle to which they were so committed, but I don't think I've ever had better houseguests.

The next day they were leaving for Timothy Leary's farm and invited me to join them. I was ready to get into the car when I realized that they were all tripping on acid. "Honk when you get to the border." One of them laughed. That's when I decided to stay home. Visiting Timothy Leary's farm in 1967 with the Grateful Dead would probably have been one of the most mind-blowing experiences of my life, but maybe that was the trouble. It was fun sharing their world for a couple of days, but I wasn't quite sure I wanted to jump down the rabbit hole. My life was crazy enough; I wasn't sure I could take more, and I was probably right.

Roger's wild lifestyle was slowly but surely consuming my life. I couldn't trust leaving him alone. One weekend when I went to Toronto to visit my parents, Roger called England without telling me. When I got the phone bill it was $347. That was more than a month's rent in 1967. Neither one of us could pay it, and we lost our phone service.

He was also getting more violent. One night, in a drunken rage, he had gone to his ex-wife's apartment, and when she refused to let him in he tried to break down the door. He was arrested and thrown in jail. I bailed him out but for once I didn't believe his bullshit about what had happened. I couldn't understand why he was still obsessed with his ex-wife and it made me very worried; the violence was terrifying.

Then his rage exploded at home. I'm not sure I knew what it was about at the time and I certainly don't remember now, but I do remember him tramping down the stairs yelling about something, stopping long enough to pull a phone cord out of the wall, pounding his fist through the wall, and breaking a couple of chairs.

The next day one of his friends came over with a bottle of Irish whisky, Roger's favourite. I knew if I didn't do something, they would drink the whole bottle and I would have to deal with his rage again. If I poured it down the kitchen sink, they would be furious. So I started drinking. I don't know how much I drank but I drank it down fast. When I finished the bottle, they went off to a local bar called the Swiss Hut.

Once the nausea passed and the drunken stupor set in, I decided I would show Roger what it was like to deal with me when I was a drunk and out of control. I got up and started the two-block trip down Hutchison Street to the Swiss Hut. It was as if everything—the street, the sidewalk, and the houses—was in a thick fog. I had never been so drunk. I had to concentrate to put one foot in front of the other. When I got there, they were sitting at a table with a bunch of pretty young McGill students. I sat down and said to the waitress in a loud voice: "Call the cops, I'm drunk." Everyone but Roger thought it was hilarious.

Roger decided to get me out of there just in time for me to puke my guts out on the sidewalk. Then he walked me home, took me upstairs to the bedroom, and left. I had to vomit again and managed to get to the bathroom. When I woke up at dawn, I was lying on the hallway floor and his dog Pele was licking my face with concern. Roger was still not home. I was sick in bed for three days from alcohol poisoning.

That's when I decided to leave. I couldn't admit that I was leaving to save myself from Roger but I think he knew. My excuse was that I was graduating soon and couldn't find a job as a journalist in Montreal. I had been writing for *Midnight* magazine, a supermarket tabloid. While the job paid well, I hated it and Roger was horrified that I would stoop so low to make a living. When I graduated from McGill, I applied for a full-time job at a private radio station writing news, where many of my male *Daily* friends were working.

"We don't hire girls in the newsroom," the producer told me. "The men swear in the newsroom and wouldn't be comfortable with a girl."

"I don't give a shit if they swear," I responded. And then I was doubly damned not only for being a woman but a foul-mouthed woman at that. Quebec's human rights charter was not passed until 1975; at the time, discrimination against women was still legal.

Roger didn't want me to leave but he had promised to support me in whatever I wanted to do in my life, and he did. I think he knew then that I wasn't coming back.

I MOVED TO TORONTO in early October 1967, and stayed with my parents and younger brother, Alvin, in their apartment on Bathurst Street in Forest Hill. Alvin and I shared a bedroom, which was a bit of a drag, but dealing with my father was something else altogether. I was twenty-two years old and had been living a bohemian lifestyle. There was no way I was going to listen to Jack's rants about how long I was staying out or what I was doing, and there was no way he was going to put up with me living an independent life under his roof. I also now had the particular arrogance of a sixties radical. Whatever my parents knew, I knew better.

"Just because you're older doesn't make you wiser," I would say.

Our arguments were driving everyone crazy, even Jack. After a particularly vicious fight, he gave me a month's rent so I could get my own place. He had recovered quickly from the bankruptcy in Quebec. Once back in Toronto, he had gotten a job selling windows. Using a combination of humour and intimidation, he was an outstanding salesman. I was furious that he was throwing me out, even though I was relieved to be going.

Besides the arguments with Jack, the main thing I remember about moving back home was my relationship with Alvin. He was almost nineteen and in grade thirteen. We used to laugh a lot. "My sister thinks her clothes hang from the floor up," he would tell his friends. Alvin was already smoking dope so we did that together, too. One weekend when my parents were away, we threw a party at the apartment with his friends and my friends, most of whom were expat Montrealers. The adult closeness Alvin and I developed then has lasted for a lifetime. To this day, he remains my best friend.

Leonard and his first wife, Maureen, had a place on Markham Street in Toronto's Annex, which was pretty run-down in those days. When Leonard and Maureen broke up later that year, he and I moved to a much bigger one-bedroom apartment on St. George Street near the University of Toronto. Every month we'd trade places — one would sleep on the bed and one on the couch.

I think part of the reason I had such a close relationship with my brothers was because we had formed a bond in our childhood in trying to defend ourselves against Jack. I would not have survived these later years without them.

Seven

NO WAY HOME

WITHIN A YEAR I decided to move to New York City. I found Toronto really boring and became disillusioned with journalism rather quickly.

Both the anti-war and the student movements were growing in leaps and bounds, and the assassination of Martin Luther King sparked uprisings in Black communities across the country, strengthening the Black Power movement. The youth revolution in France in May and June of 1968 had a major impact on the New Left, transforming what started as a movement for democracy and against war into a more general revolutionary movement that raised questions about capitalism, imperialism, and colonialism. New York was one of the centres of radical change in politics, lifestyle, music, and the arts. I was still an American citizen so there was no legal barrier to the move and my aunts were glad to put me up. Even though I didn't get directly involved in activism, my experiences in New York shaped many of my political views in the years to come.

I arrived in Brooklyn in the fall of 1968. My first job was at Christina Gorby, the coolest dress store in the East Village. Greenwich Village had been the centre of the Beat movement and the jazz revival, and now it was the centre of the folk scene. But it was the East Village that was hip in 1968. It had an otherworldly feeling. The air seemed heavier and darker. Even during the day, it seemed like night. In the beautiful memoir of her relationship with the artist Robert Mapplethorpe, singer and poet Patti Smith talks about "the yellow filtered light of the East Village." Living there in the broken-down tenements filled with drug dealers, artists, and hippies was out of the question for a middle-class girl like me, but hanging out in the delis on 2nd Avenue and the bars on 8th Street, and going to concerts at the Fillmore East, was the centre of my social life.

Christina Gorby was a great introduction to the East Village. The store sold designer clothes at fairly low prices so everyone who was anyone bought their clothes there. Among the patrons were Janis Joplin and Jimi Hendrix, both of whom were East Village denizens. The other girls were wonderful gossips. They loved Hendrix and hated Joplin with equal passion, both opinions based on how friendly the rock stars were to the sales girls.

One day after work one of my friends invited me to join her for dinner at a 2nd Avenue deli. Just after we turned the corner from 8th Street, she saw some guys she knew. It was two of the Yippies, a counter-culture political group that was famous for its antics during protests at the August 1968

Democratic National Convention in Chicago. The protests turned violent. Abbie Hoffman and Jerry Rubin would be charged as part of the Chicago Seven in one of the most famous trials in U.S. history. They were already legendary. They were also hyper and full of themselves, and it was hard to understand what they were talking about. But I did understand their attitude toward me, which was that I was not much more interesting to them than a piece of meat. Sexism was pretty pervasive in those days, but they were particularly obnoxious.

New York provided a great place for sexual exploration. In the last few months I was in Toronto, I wondered, if men could feel free to sleep with whomever they wanted, why couldn't women? In Toronto, men looked askance at "easy" women but New York was an entirely different story. Greenwich Village was one big pickup scene. It seemed that every café and every bar was populated with men and women on the make. Without much effort, I could have had sex with a different man every night. I didn't go quite that far but I certainly made up for lost time.

One evening, I went to a coffee house and a very handsome and charming young Black man sat with me. His name was Wheat. He walked me home and kissed me good night.

Wheat was a lovely man in so many ways: intelligent, talented, kind, funny, and loving. He came to New York from the South. He didn't have much of an education and had a hard time finding a job that interested him. He was an artist, too. He sold his drawings on the street in the Village and they were good.

I remember he had the most extraordinary touch, light and gentle.

"Where did you learn to touch like that?" I asked.

"You won't believe me."

"Yes, I will." The truth was I believed pretty well everything people told me. It's not that I was naive; it's just that I always assumed the best about anyone I liked and I'm still like that.

"My dad was a pickpocket. He taught me how to do it. You had to be so light-fingered that the mark wouldn't notice a thing until he needed some money. My dad worked the subway platform during rush hour. He'd be long gone by the time his mark realized the wallet was gone."

"So you're a pickpocket?"

"Nah, I hate crowds. Can't be a pickpocket if you hate crowds. Kind of like being a swimmer if you hate water."

His only other option was to work in a factory, which he didn't want to do. Somehow he had money, but I knew better than to get into the details.

It was through my relationship with Wheat that I started to understand racism. Walking along the streets of the Village, people would ask me for directions, even though I was the woman. When I would refer the question to him, they would walk away. It was bizarre. When I would get mad, Wheat would put his arm around my shoulder and say gently with a look of love in his eyes, "That's the way it is, Judy. It's only because you're from Canada that you even notice it. I don't let it bug me." It bugged me a lot.

Then one day, Wheat disappeared. I had never been to his place so I didn't know where he lived, but I did know where he and his friends hung out so I went looking for him. They told me he was in jail. He had been busted for running heroin to Harlem. I had figured he was probably selling pot or hash, but heroin, that was a different story. I had a crisis of conscience. Running heroin to the ghetto was something I disapproved of politically and morally. But how could I judge him? Even as a woman, the opportunities for me were so much greater than for him as a Black man. How could I judge what he did to make a living?

"We didn't have the money for bail," his friend told me.

"How much?" I asked.

"One hundred dollars."

"Why didn't you come to me?"

"I didn't think you'd bail him out," he replied glumly.

"I'm going out with him. Of course I would bail him out if I could," I said.

Looking down, he just shook his head. At that moment I realized that they thought I was just seeing him for the sex. And maybe he thought that, too. Or maybe he didn't want me to find out what he was into. I was more upset by that than the discovery that he was selling heroin. How could my perception of our relationship be so different from his?

Later the friend came to my apartment to pick up the money. The next day Wheat came over to thank me.

He kissed me and hugged me. "I love you, Judy. I think we should get married."

I was only twenty-two. I wasn't thinking about getting married; I was just beginning to feel my way in the world.

"I'm really flattered, Wheat, but I'm not ready to get married. I don't even know if I want to get married at all.

I like you a lot and I want to keep going out with you but marriage, no."

I don't know if it was because he was offended or ashamed, but we broke up soon after. My experience with Wheat made me understand the impact of racism. From that moment on, fighting bigotry has always been central to my politics.

AFTER MY EXPERIENCE in Toronto, I didn't want to work in journalism, but I was a good writer so I got a job at the Centre for Handicapped Children at Columbia University translating academic articles into a newsletter. Columbia was also the centre of the student movement. In the spring of 1968, Students for a Democratic Society (SDS) had organized the largest and most effective student strike in U.S. history. More than a million students walked out of school and shut down campuses from coast to coast. Most of the national media focus was on the shutdown at Columbia University led by the inter-racial alliance of SDS chairperson Mark Rudd and the Student Afro Society activists. So naturally, I gravitated to Columbia SDS.

I attended an SDS meeting in preparation for what became a famous national conference in the spring of 1969. For reasons I didn't fully understand at the time, the meeting of almost a thousand people was dominated by ferocious arguments that ended in fistfights. It turned out that this meeting was the beginning of the emergence of the radical political group the Weathermen, which soon split from SDS and began a series of bombings and other violent acts. They believed that a revolution was imminent; all they needed to do was spur it on through violent dramatic actions. At the time they called themselves the Weathermen from the Bob Dylan song "Subterranean Homesick Blues." But I had no interest in joining a group that solved its problems with fists, let alone bombs. Instead I started gravitating toward the more hippie side of sixties radicalization, living life for the experience.

NEW YORK CITY was violent in those years and sexual harassment was rampant. We didn't have a name for it then, but if you walked alone at night in New York City, some man was always exposing himself, grabbing you, or at the very least explicitly hitting on you. Most women I knew never walked alone at night but I wasn't willing to restrict myself that way. I learned quickly that the best way to deal with the harassment was to make a scene: there were always people around and New Yorkers, bless them, rarely mind their own business.

"Put it back in your pants!" I would yell at the flasher. "Take your fucking hands off me!" I would holler if someone touched or grabbed me. Once someone said, "I love your thighs." I answered, "If I could take them off, I'd lend them to you." Look tough, act tough, make a scene. Unlike most women, I wasn't afraid of confrontation. Confrontation was like mother's milk to me, or rather father's milk. What I experienced in New York might have been shocking to a born and bred Toronto girl, but I had been subjected to flashers ever since I rode the New York subway alone as a teenager visiting my mother's family. Usually I would just get up and walk away. I was determined not to let the harassment limit my freedom, but no doubt it affected me more deeply than I realized.

As it turned out, my apartment was much more dangerous than the streets. One night in late August, I woke up to a scream so shattering I can still hear it today. A moment later, there was a shot and then quiet. I called the police.

"You don't have to give us your name," the operator said. It was several years after the Kitty Genovese killing in Queens, an infamous case in which many neighbours observed the knife assault but did nothing to help the victim for fear of being murdered themselves. Now New York emergency services provided anonymity for callers to encourage the reporting of crimes. But I was from Toronto. Why wouldn't I give them my name? Didn't the police have to get into the building? Better I should buzz them in than have them break down the door.

"There's been a shooting upstairs, please hurry," I whispered into the phone.

Suddenly I realized one escape route for the shooter would be down the fire escape and through my window. Quickly making up my bed, I hid in the closet until the police arrived. My mind was racing. *What will I do if he does come into my apartment? Will I make a run for it? That doesn't make sense. He isn't looking for me; he'll just go out the door. No, I'll hold my breath so he won't know I'm here. And why would he care if he knows I am here? I can't see him. But he'll know that I'm hiding and that I know what he did. I could sneak a peak. Staying in the closet, I'm a sitting duck. Maybe I should make a run for it.*

At last the buzzer rang and I stepped out to let the cops in. I heard them trooping up the stairs and then silence. Apparently when they arrived, the gunman was standing over the body waiting for them. He was her boyfriend.

The next morning the tiny lobby was full of people asking, "Who called the police?" They had all heard the scream and the shot, and I was the only one who called the police. That day, I decided to leave New York. The city was very heavy, and I had had enough of the violence, the racism, the sexism, and the harassment. I wanted to go somewhere a young, independent woman could be free.

Eight

"WALK QUICKLY, THERE IS DANGER"

AT THE END OF the sixties and into the seventies a division developed in the youth culture, with some people exploring alternative lifestyles through drugs, travel, music, Eastern religion, and self-help and others moving into more radical politics. For a while I was more into the hippie side.

Lots of young people were backpacking around Europe, hitching rides and staying at cheap hotels. I decided that I would join them. It was part of the hippie youth culture to travel with little money and less luggage, without an agenda or a goal. It would allow me to let go of whatever middle-class values still restricted me. Needless to say, my father was not thrilled with the idea that I was taking off on a trip through Europe by myself, but because I wasn't asking him for money there was little he could do to stop me.

Starting in London, I grabbed a ride to Morocco with two guys in a Volkswagen van, but got out in Barcelona when their demands for sex became too annoying—a constant hazard for a woman travelling alone. After a wild month in Spain, I headed for Greece. Greece's haven for hippie travellers was Matala in southern Crete. It may not have been as spectacular as other parts of Crete, but it had a beautiful white sand beach with a village at one end and caves dating from the Neolithic era at the other. The caves were used as tombs in the first and second centuries. In the twentieth century, they were a perfect place to set up camp.

Travellers in Matala talked about going to Israel, one of the few places around the Mediterranean where you could get work. Israel was a place of great romance for North American Jews. Every year at the end of the Passover Seder we say, "Next year in Jerusalem." The story is that the Jews, so viciously enslaved by the Egyptians, were led out of Egypt by Moses to wander in the desert and that someday we would return to claim our land. While my father was hostile to religion, he wanted to be part of the Jewish tradition and Israel was an important part of that. He became a top fundraiser for the United Jewish Appeal, which raised money for Israel. He travelled there on a mission in 1956 and loved it. I hadn't heard much to counter his enthusiasm, and in 1970 there wasn't a lot of criticism of Israel from the New Left.

On the other hand, Phillip, an American I met in Greece, had spent some time there and was very critical. He was a Jewish American and one of the first really political people I met on that trip.

"It's a police state," he warned. "If you're a Jew and you hang out with Arabs, they'll follow you everywhere and harass you. The only way to get hash there is from the Arabs, so you'll have to hang out with them. Plus they're the coolest people in the place. So watch out."

"C'mon, you're exaggerating. I've been to Spain and Greece, both run by dictatorships, and there was nothing like that. Israel is a democracy; how bad could it be?"

"You'll see," he said, shrugging his shoulders, raising his eyebrows, and nodding his head knowingly.

I ENTERED ISRAEL through the port of Jaffa. As soon as I got off the boat, the magic of the Holy Land hit me—and, simultaneously, the shocking aggression of the people.

At this point, the North American narrative portrayed Israel as a plucky little country that had successfully stood up to Great Britain and then to its bully Arab neighbours. In 1967, the story went, the Israelis had not only saved themselves from destruction but also taken over some land from their neighbours, presumably to better defend themselves. Of course I also knew the myth of the Exodus, both the biblical liberation from Egypt and the modern story of the ship that brought post-Holocaust Jewish immigrants to Palestine, so brilliantly mythologized in Leon Uris's blockbuster novel *Exodus* and the 1960 film of the same name starring Paul Newman. On top of that, Israel had the kibbutz, a collective farm where everyone did the work and everyone got the benefit, where men and women were equal and children were raised by the community—a socialist paradise, or so we were told.

It was true that men and women did many of the same jobs on the kibbutz and that Golda Meir, a rare female political leader, was prime minister, but for a young woman the streets of Israel were worse than the streets of New York. Israeli guys were incredibly aggressive and sexist. I felt more at risk than ever before.

The racism really bothered me. In Jerusalem, there was very little mixing between Arabs and Jews. Arabs would sit at the back of the bus. In 1955, in Montgomery, Alabama, a young Black woman named Rosa Parks refused to sit in the back of the bus, thus defying the segregation laws and sparking a twelve-month bus boycott by the Black community. The Montgomery bus boycott became a central symbol of the U.S. civil rights movement. There was no law that required Arabs to sit in the back of the bus, but they always did, and no Jewish Israeli ever sat next to them. I went out of my way to sit in the back next to the Arabs.

A couple of weeks into my trip, I met a very nice elderly Arab man who spoke fluent English. Farooq was in his early seventies and he loved meeting young travellers so he could practise his English. He told us stories of the land before the state of Israel was established, but he never showed any hostility to Israelis and certainly not to Jews. We were both friends with Jeremy and Laura, a young American couple who were staying in one of the ancient hotels in the old city. It was March and Jerusalem was cool that time of year. The cheap hotels had portable gas heaters for the comfort of their guests. One night the heater in Jeremy and Laura's room blew up. The explosion killed Laura and put Jeremy in the hospital. Farooq and I went to visit him with heavy hearts.

When we arrived at the hospital, two security guards

walked up to us, said something in Hebrew to Farooq, and took his arm.

"They want me to go through a back door to be searched," Farooq said in a quiet voice.

"He's with me," I said to the guard. "We're visiting a friend together."

"Sorry, miss," the guard said politely in English. "It is policy. All Arabs must be searched before entering the hospital. I hope you understand; we have to be careful." They were still at war with their neighbour states and therefore suspicious of any Arab, even those who were living in Israel.

"I do *not* understand," I said. "I'll go with him then."

"No, you won't," he said more firmly, as one of the guards escorted Farooq while the other one stood in my way.

"Do not worry, Judy," Farooq said, indicating that I should stop protesting. "We will meet in Jeremy's room."

I, who had been in the country for only a couple of weeks, was allowed to walk right into the hospital. Farooq, who had lived in Jerusalem his entire life and whose parents and grandparents had also lived there, was forced to go into a back room where he would be searched and humiliated. I was horrified. He was an old man and one of the most pacific people I had ever met. He had come to the hospital with food to comfort and help a young friend get through what was probably the worst moment in his short life.

We didn't tell Jeremy about what had happened, but after we left I expressed my outrage to Farooq.

He just shook his head sadly. "It's just the way it is, Judy. There is nothing we can do."

It was the exact same response I had gotten from Wheat

about racism in New York. Thereafter, I spent a lot more time talking to Arabs and learning about their perspective on what had happened to what they called Palestine. I was confused about the conflicting stories, but it became clear to me that it was the Arabs who were facing discrimination and the Jewish Israelis who were inflicting it. My anger at the political situation made me forget the warning about what happens to Jews who hang out with Arabs.

THE REASON I WENT to Israel was to find work; by this time, I was running low on funds. I decided my best bet was a kibbutz. Ein Gev was in Galilee in northern Israel. It had been founded by Americans so the kibbutzniks [members of the kibbutz] spoke English. I was also told that hash was easy to come by at Ein Gev, which wasn't the case at other kibbutzim.

There were a lot of young American Jews who had come to Israel in order to volunteer on a kibbutz. The Six-Day War in 1967 had had a big impact on youth in North America and to a lesser extent in Europe. Little Israel had defeated what looked to us like an Arab Goliath. Moreover, the kibbutz seemed like one of the only real collectivist experiments in the world. We all slept together in co-ed dorms, which was pretty remarkable in those days. Most of the kibbutz members were white American Jews, except for the kitchen staff who were Sephardic Jews mainly from North Africa. The only Arabs I met on the kibbutz were dealing hash.

The land was beautiful, surrounded by mountains. Ein Gev was located on the incredibly lush plateau of the Golan

Heights, one of the most beautiful parts of Israel. We stayed in cabins, woke up at 6 a.m. to work the fields picking oranges, and in the afternoon we worked in the kitchens. The kibbutz was far from the socialist paradise it claimed to be. It's true that men and women worked together in the fields and in the kitchen, but the worst jobs were given to Sephardic Jews from North Africa and the Middle East. The racism went beyond Arabs to dark-skinned Jews. They got the more menial jobs and were not even members of the kibbutz, but hired help.

I stayed on the kibbutz for about a month, then decided to go back to Greece. I was anxious to get out of Israel, which I found militarist, sexist, and racist. Everything I valued about being Jewish didn't seem to be there. Some part of me liked the fact that everyone—the cops, the farmers, the firefighters—was Jewish, but I didn't feel at home there.

The kibbutz volunteers threw me a party the evening before I was leaving. Needless to say, there was a lot of hash. I also got some from a local Arab dealer because you couldn't buy it in Greece. I was confident that the Israelis wouldn't care if I smuggled it out of the country and that the Greeks would never search a woman. Nevertheless I needed a place to hide it. Like most hippie girls, I didn't wear a bra but I packed one, in case I needed it for just such a purpose or if I had to look straight. I couldn't find my bra so I put the seven grams of hash in a Kotex pad, inserted it in my underwear, and headed off.

As soon as I arrived at the port, I knew I was in trouble. The guy at the entrance took my passport and said my name out loud. A man in a suit came over and asked me to follow him. I don't think I'd ever seen anyone in Israel wear a suit. I had only a few minutes to plan my strategy.

He took me into a small room, where two men searched my backpack. They were customs officials, not in uniform. They looked everywhere I could have hidden the drugs, even turning the oranges and bread around to see if there were any holes in them. My hair was long and frizzy, and I was wearing Indian clothes that were fashionable among travellers. Even though I looked like a stoned-out hippie, I decided to play it straight.

"What are you looking for?" I asked, smiling. "Bombs, microfiche?" I laughed.

They didn't laugh but looked at me with considerable hostility while they questioned me about my time in Jerusalem. They knew everywhere I had been. Phillip's warnings about hanging out with Arabs came back to me, along with all the stories I had heard on my travels about body searches, long waits for trials, but most of all how they confiscated people's passports. Even worse, I knew I'd have to call my parents if I was arrested. My father would come for sure. Jack was Israel's top fundraiser in Toronto. He would try to use his influence and, failing that, try to bully someone into freeing me. That was a fate worse than going to jail.

When they couldn't find anything in the pack, a young woman came into the room.

"Follow her," the suit said to me.

"Why?" I asked.

"She is going to search your body," he replied.

"What? I am Jewish and a college graduate! I've travelled all over Europe and I've never had a body search. This

94

is supposed to be my homeland! How can you treat me like this?" In an instant I turned from compliant, curious tourist into entitled potential immigrant.

The woman asked me to undress. I slowly started undressing. The entire time I continued my rant — "I have never been humiliated like this!" — until I was down to my underwear and my bandaged foot. That morning, I had stepped on a piece of glass and the kibbutz doctor had treated the gash.

"Take off the bandage," she said.

"You want me to take off this bandage? Then you get on the phone and call an ambulance! I am not risking an infection for this stupidity."

I figured I had nothing to lose, so I decided to make her life as difficult as possible. In addition, a trip in an ambulance might give me the opportunity to ditch the hash. It's hard to believe that a twenty-four-year-old woman with little experience of border guards would consciously plan such a strategy, but I had learned a lot from my father about dealing with petty bureaucrats and border guards.

"Okay," she said, her voice slightly shaking. "Take off your pants."

I turned and looked her straight in the eye. "I'm on my period and I am not taking off my pants. I have been humiliated quite enough." I made it clear that if my underwear was coming off, she would have to remove them.

"Okay," she said. "Get dressed."

I had to be sure not to show any relief so I kept yelling at her, at the guy in the suit, at the guys who searched my bags.

"Are you sure?" her boss asked her. "Did you look everywhere?"

"Yes," she lied. They knew I had the hash. It was well known that the Arab dealers would sell to tourists, inform on them, then get the hash back as well as their money. I was lucky she was younger than I was and easily intimidated.

Looking back, I realize this was the first time in my adult life that I had dissociated from any feelings of fear. This ability to exercise complete emotional detachment allowed me to quickly and coolly assess a tense and threatening situation, to stand up to authorities, and to keep going, which is what I did.

AFTER ISRAEL I DECIDED to set out upon what is now called "the hippie trail." Travelling alone from Turkey to Iran, Afghanistan, and India, I was confronted again and again with dangerous and hostile situations. Fellow travellers had warned me that it was too dangerous for a woman to do the trail by herself, but I didn't listen.

My first stop was Istanbul. Someone suggested that it would be easier, safer, and more scenic to take a boat along the south coast of the Black Sea rather than a bus across Turkey. The events of the days that followed wiped out the memory of what was likely a lovely boat trip.

When we arrived at the port, I got on an old rickety bus that was supposed to drive through the mountains directly to Doğubayazıt, the last Turkish town on the highway to Iran. From there I could get a train that would go to Tehran. I wanted to arrive in India before the rainy season in the summer.

Men and women sat separately on the bus, the women

on one side and the men on the other. Since no one spoke English or seemed very friendly, all I could do was look out the window. I smiled at the woman next to me, but she didn't return my smile, just looked down. The scenery was beautiful as we travelled through the mountains, but the villages we passed through were terribly poor, made up mostly of rundown shacks. The only toilet facilities were holes in the ground, covered in flies.

I was dressed very modestly in loose Indian clothes. Nevertheless I was an object of curiosity, especially for the men. Most people in this part of the world had never seen a Western woman before.

As night fell, the driver made an unscheduled stop in a village to rest. After a couple of passengers got off the bus, the driver started packing up as if he intended to spend the night there. A group of men began gathering around the bus. When they saw me, they started tapping on the windows and knocking on the door. I went up to the driver to indicate that I was frightened. At first he just laughed. Then they started pounding on the windows, and I turned around and noticed the looks of concern on the faces of the women. An unaccustomed fear was growing in my belly.

"Please, let's go," I said, pointing ahead. "No stop here."

"No problem," he said.

Pointing to the men now banging on the bus, I replied, "Big problem, big problem," miming with my arms.

I went back to my fellow travellers, asking one of them to intervene. A man went up to the driver and asked him to continue the journey, but the driver ignored him, too. Then the pounding got louder and more violent.

Finally the driver realized we were in danger and managed to pull away.

After about two weeks in Tehran, a modern city where lots of students I met spoke English, I took the train to Mashhad, where I was told I could get a ride to Herat, Afghanistan.

Mashhad is a beautiful, ancient city. Today it is a big tourist town, but back then it was a sleepy village. After checking into a small hotel near the train station, I immediately went out for a walk. I saw a group of people in a nearby park and wandered over to see what they were doing. Before I got very close, someone threw a stone at me and then more people started throwing stones. At first I was stunned. It was the middle of the twentieth century and I was dressed modestly, yet I was being stoned like a harlot in ancient times. It didn't take me long to start running, and run I did, as fast as I could to my hotel.

I checked to make sure I wasn't hurt and then tried to calm down and figure out how I was going to get out of there safely. About an hour later, there was a knock on my door. When I opened it a friendly man said in broken English, "So sorry, miss, so sorry." He pointed to a badly beaten young man on the ground next to him. The young man was the one who had started throwing the stones. His face was black and blue, and from the way he was holding himself I assumed his body had taken an even worse beating. The beating was meant as an apology to me, but seeing the young man on the ground made me sick. I couldn't wait to get out of the country.

THE BUS LEFT MASHHAD early in the morning and arrived in Herat, the second-biggest city in Afghanistan, in mid-afternoon. Afghanistan was still a peaceful place in 1970. It was near the end of Mohammed Zahir Shah's forty-year reign. During this time, Afghanistan was a relatively open society for travellers. Hash was legal and plentiful so lots of hippies stopped there. In fact the main role of Afghan border guards seemed to be to stop travellers from carrying Afghani hash into Iran where they would be arrested or worse. Drug laws were so lax in Kabul that there was a pharmacy known to many that sold heroin over the counter.

Afghanistan had good relationships with Western countries through the United Nations but very little contact with Western tourists other than hippies. It was, however, quite religious. Unlike in Turkey and most of Iran, women there were often veiled. It was the first time I saw women wearing the burka. Women appeared very little in public and certainly never interacted with travellers, but the Afghani men were polite, kind, and hospitable. Much less influenced by the West, they were obviously proud of their culture. They invited travellers to share their food and to talk in whatever way we could given the language differences, but they were neither solicitous nor aggressive. The country had a calm, quiet beauty. I loved it there and have felt heartsick about its tragic history ever since.

I remember an evening in Herat, sitting around a fire with a few travellers and a group of Afghani men dressed in tribal clothes. They were cooking meat on an open fire. For the first time since I had arrived in Istanbul two months before, I felt safe. I stayed in Herat until I was able to get a ride to Kabul.

Kabul is said to be more than 3,500 years old. Located in a narrow valley between the Hindu Kush mountains, it was a key location for trade along the Silk Road. Running short of money, I arranged through a wire to my mother to have some money transferred to a bank in Kabul. I had left some money in my account in Toronto with a letter allowing my mother access to it. It turned out that one of the ways the Afghan bank made money in those days was to hold transfers for a while, a week, two weeks, one never knew. I was stuck in Kabul with little or no money. Luckily the owner of the hotel agreed I could stay there and pay him once the funds came through. My situation was a common one.

Another stroke of luck was that Karen, a Canadian woman I had travelled with from Spain to Greece, showed up in Kabul with her boyfriend about a week after I got there. After all I had gone through, it was so good to see friends and a huge relief to be with a woman.

One day Karen and I were taking a walk in downtown Kabul. I had a feeling that something was wrong. Suddenly a man came up to us and quietly said, "Walk quickly, there is danger. The mullahs have come down from the mountains. It is dangerous. Leave!"

As we made our way back to the hotel, we saw a group of robed holy men chanting and marching toward us. The mullahs were conservative Muslim scholars who did not think women should appear in public without the burka. Perhaps these men were organizing for the Islamic revolution that would follow in the coming years.

Despite that incident the relative safety of Kabul allowed me to relax and I realized I was quite depressed. My energy had flagged. I had diarrhea off and on. I figured it was the upset stomach that made me so tired, but I hadn't had sex or even desired sex since I had left Israel.

I thought a night of passion would do me good, so when a tall, handsome, blond American man flirted with me in the hotel restaurant I responded even though I didn't feel attracted to him. His name was Paul and he was from Seattle. He was travelling from India.

"I was busted for dope there," he said. "Now I just want to get home as soon as I can. I'm waiting for some money from home and staying with friends here."

There were a lot of Westerners living in Kabul, most of them junkies who could access heroin from the drugstore and live a decent lifestyle. He was staying with them on the outskirts of the city.

He had a small pickup truck that he had borrowed from one of his friends. I got in the cab of the truck and we went back to his place where we had sex. I felt nothing, no pleasure, no fear, no sadness, nothing. I pretended to enjoy myself but he knew what was happening. He wouldn't talk to me on the drive back to the hotel but said he would pick me up later for a lamb roast that evening.

When he came back, he seemed really angry.

"Let's talk about it," I offered.

"No sweat," Paul responded but I could see that wasn't true.

When we got to the campsite, he went to his room while I sat around the fire and partook in the copious amounts of hash being circulated. At some point he came out and sat on the opposite side of the large circle around the fire. I was very stoned and not sure what to do about him. The scene was already surreal. About fifty hippies surrounded a giant fire with a full lamb roasting over the flames. The crackle of the fire and the small explosions when the fat hit the flames, combined with the delicious smell of roasting lamb, triggered all kinds of contradictory senses. Most if not all of us were stoned on hash or heroin. The group's intense drugged state hovered over the circle.

Should I get up and join him? I thought, trying unsuccessfully to make eye contact. *Maybe I should explain what bad shape I'm in so he doesn't take it personally, but I don't even know this guy and right now he seems kind of hostile. But he's a nice person; he wouldn't hurt me. You're being paranoid, for Christ's sake. Get up and talk to him.*

Before I could move, he got up, uncurled to his full six feet, and started to stride toward me. I hesitated, not sure what to do. I got up but still didn't move from my spot—something was holding me there. If I had been more myself, I probably would have started walking toward him, but instead I just stood up and kept looking at the fire, catching him in the corner of my eye.

Then, I felt a wind at my back.

I turned around and looked behind me.

A knife in that tree. A hunting knife. It wasn't there before, was it? I thought. I looked again and then walked over to the tree and put my hand on the knife handle. It was vibrating. *Oh my god, he must have thrown that knife. Was he throwing it at me, or thinking about throwing it at me? I gotta get outta here.*

If I had taken a few steps toward him, I might have been dead or certainly severely injured.

I went to the street and got a pedicab back to the hotel. I was shaken, more shaken than I had been on the entire trip. I guess the fear of what could have happened was great enough to break through the depression.

I told Karen what happened and she said that I should stick with them for the rest of my time in Kabul. I didn't want to go to the police. Travellers never knew what would happen if they went to the police.

Paul never showed his face again in the cafés or hotels. Karen's boyfriend said a lot of people, by whom he meant men, travelling east to west were pretty fucked up and that I should keep a distance. I was traumatized by the experience and wanted to get out of Kabul as soon as possible. I went back to the bank, this time promising myself I wouldn't leave until they handed me the money. They did.

TWO DAYS AFTER the knife attack, I set out for India. I was no longer having fun. This was a perilous journey where every decision could mean life or death. There were no more philosophical discussions, no more drug-induced mind wanderings. When I met a Westerner, the discussion was strictly limited to obtaining information: a safe place to stay, to eat, to sleep. I had started writing in a journal in Turkey, something I hadn't really done since childhood. I remember writing, "A climb to every summit is rewarded with a better view of dawn."

It was in India that I finally saw the dawn.

What seemed to me to be the silence and submission of the women in Turkey, Iran, and Afghanistan gave way to the animated women in India dressed in their colourful saris, chatting, laughing, and curious about me. Men treated me with respect, telling me how much courage it must take for a woman to travel alone. It was almost as if I were watching a movie that suddenly changed from black and white to colour, like that scene in *The Wizard of Oz* when Dorothy leaves Kansas and arrives in Oz.

After a couple of weeks in the mountains, feeling somewhat recovered from fatigue and depression, I headed south to Amritsar and from there I travelled to Delhi. On the way to Amritsar, the bus I was on made an unscheduled stop. Everyone got out and the women invited me to sit with them. None of them spoke English, but somehow I managed to communicate that I was from Canada and travelling alone. They showed me their jewellery and offered me food. I was falling in love with India.

When I arrived in Delhi, the crowds and the summer heat were overwhelming. Here, for the first time, there were real tourists and fancy hotels. I was ready for a little bit of luxury even if I couldn't afford it. Arriving at a hotel recommended by other travellers, I discovered that I had to share a room with a man. His name was Alan, and luckily he was from Ottawa. Given my recent experiences I was worried I'd have to fight off his advances, but he was polite and kind. What's more, he had been in India for a while, so he knew the ropes. In the end, he helped save my life.

Alan suggested that I go to Calcutta, which was even more crowded and impoverished than Delhi. But then I got really sick. It started with a fever and diarrhea. At first it didn't seem that different from the stomach flu, but it got worse—much worse. In the forty-degree heat I felt as if I was burning up, and then I started shitting water. Dysentery was my roommate's diagnosis. He also told me that cholera starts the same way, and the disease can be fatal. I asked him how you knew the difference.

"Cholera doesn't stop," he said.

I had never been so sick. There was a moment when I thought I might die. And in that moment I made a promise. Maybe it was a prayer. Later in my life, when I embraced Marxism and rejected all religion, I thought of it as an epiphany, a realization of how I would spend the rest of my life.

If I live through this, I promised myself, *I will devote my life to changing the world.*

The poverty I'd seen on the trip had so deeply disturbed me that I was already thinking about getting active politically and fighting U.S. imperialism, which I saw as the source of most of the misery in these countries. The terrible oppression I had felt as a woman was also a factor. I had come to realize that the oppression of women was a social and cultural issue, not just an individual problem.

These experiences would guide the rest of my life.

III

DOWN BUT NOT OUT

1970–1985

Nine

THE REVOLUTIONARY SEVENTIES

I ARRIVED BACK IN CANADA on July 21, a few hours before I left Tokyo, in that weird way of crossing the international date line. Somehow the topsy-turvy time was a metaphor for my travels. Too sick to stay in India much longer, I had called my parents, asking if they would pay for an airline ticket home. My illness overcame my pride. Much to my amazement, my mother suggested a ticket to Japan, which I had always wanted to visit, and then Vancouver where my brother Leonard, who was now living in BC, could pick me up.

When I arrived at Vancouver airport, it wasn't only Leonard who came to greet me; Alvin was there with his new girlfriend, Glenna. They had decided to drive out west for a visit. After a few days in BC, I flew home to Toronto.

I first stayed with my parents, but it didn't take me long to find a room in a house with a couple of journalists I knew.

At the time, many young people lived together in communes, sharing houses, food, and company. After almost a year of constant travelling, I had terrible culture shock. On top of that I was still quite sick. After my doctor initially misdiagnosed my condition, I went to the Tropical Disease Unit at Toronto General Hospital and was diagnosed with amoebic dysentery.

After receiving treatment, I was finally ready to fulfill my promise of changing the world. The anti-war movement was at its height, succeeding in forcing peace negotiations between the U.S. and the Viet Cong. In the fall of 1970, members of the FLQ kidnapped a Quebec politician and a British diplomat, greatly escalating their tactics, which up until this time had consisted of blowing up federal symbols like mailboxes.

In response, Prime Minister Pierre Trudeau declared the War Measures Act on October 16, suspending civil liberties and creating a police state in Quebec. Five hundred people were arrested, most of whom were not affiliated with the FLQ. The youthful Left that had been protesting the Vietnam War and supporting the civil rights movement turned its attention to the Canadian state. Most Canadians supported the War Measures Act, but the Left, including the New Democratic Party under the leadership of Tommy Douglas, opposed the overreaction to a small number of FLQ activists. One of the kidnappers' demands was for the media to publish and broadcast the FLQ Manifesto, which called for an independent and socialist Quebec. While there was a lot of support for the manifesto, the kidnapping and subsequent murder of provincial cabinet minister Pierre Laporte lost the FLQ mass support in Quebec.

The War Measures Act turned my attention away from U.S. imperialism as a target of protest to Canada. I worked with my old friend Bob Chodos, and other friends in Toronto, publishing a new left-wing magazine called *Last Post*, which took a strong position against the War Measures Act.

I was also looking for a job, and the Addiction Research Foundation advertised in the newspaper for a youth drug crisis worker. I got the job working as a counsellor in the famed Trailer in Yorkville, which brought drug treatment directly to the youth who were hanging out there.

Alienated youth had become the social service challenge of the early 1970s. For several years, young people had been hanging out smoking dope and dropping acid in Yorkville. The cultural side of the sixties youth radicalism rejected consumer society and thousands of young people lived in voluntary poverty, doing drugs and often living collectively or crashing wherever they could. One of the slogans of the youth culture was "Don't trust anyone over thirty," and they didn't. It was difficult for established social services to cope with them. My job as a counsellor was to help kids come down from bad trips, refer them to a medical clinic for VD, and sometimes help them find a place to stay. I was good at it, but it didn't really engage me.

Then I found out about Grass Roots, a coalition of alternative services and political groups. As many youth groups were at the time, Grass Roots was a collective with very little structure. Decisions were made at group meetings, most of which were held at 132 Carlton Street, a commune of activists. People who worked together politically also lived together and slept with each other. We were not only challenging the political system, we were trying to create an alternate culture rejecting the strict moralism of the 1950s. Not only did I find a boyfriend, good friends, and a cause, I learned a lot about organizing and fighting for change. Before I arrived, Grass Roots had decided to set up a self-governing youth community that summer, one that would be open to all those who needed a place to stay.

In the summer of 1971, Toronto was getting ready for the invasion of thousands of transient youth from across the country. Newspapers were full of articles warning of the lack of facilities for young people who would be grabbing their backpacks, leaving home, and joining the masses of young travellers hitchhiking across North America. Grass Roots had the idea of creating an outdoor community for transient youth that would be democratically run by the people living there. The proposal was for tents that could house up to a thousand people, and the site we were recommending was the University of Toronto campus. We called it Wachea, which we thought was a Cree word for "everyone is welcome." The Cree word is actually spelled *wachiya* and means "hello." The media called it a tent city.

Wachea became the centre of cultural and political activity. Everyone wanted to be part of this new experiment. The student council tried to negotiate with the U of T administration, which was desperately pressuring the provincial government for permission to use Mercer Reformatory as the site for the tent city. Grass Roots wanted to stay at U of T because Mercer looked like the grounds of a prison (which it was), a grim warehouse-type building on a large dirt plot. And there were no facilities such as running water.

After the university officially turned down the student council, all three student organizations invited Grass Roots to occupy the circle in front of Hart House and set up our community. We set up tents, served free food, and held concerts, yoga classes, and free university classes. In many ways it resembled the Occupy protests that were established in 2011. On July 16, 1971, a judge granted an injunction forbidding us from establishing a community in front of Hart House. The police cleared us out early on a Sunday morning and were very rough with people who resisted. Twenty-one people were arrested.

After weeks of protests and negotiations, the provincial government gave us the Mercer site and on July 22 we opened Wachea there. About thirty people set up tents. Most of the young people who showed up had nowhere else to go and were not the least bit interested in our participatory democracy ideals or our free university. By the end of the first week, there were 150 campers. We provided one hot meal a day, prepared in the kitchen of the West End YMCA. The federal government provided a grant of $25,000 as part of the Opportunities for Youth program, which encouraged young people to do community work. Later I came to see these grants as an attempt to co-opt the youth movement, but at the time the funding helped pay expenses, especially setting up portable toilets and running water on the site. The grant was designed to provide salaries, but we used most of it for expenses. I got paid about $200 for the entire summer.

Nevertheless, we were middle-class and most of the kids who stayed at the camp were poor. They were just looking for a free place to stay, where they wouldn't be hassled about taking drugs, having sex, or drinking. They couldn't give a damn about our ideals.

Our idealism about a democratically run youth community was being destroyed. And there were divisions within Grass Roots among the service providers, journalists, and radical political activists. We had set out to create a self-governing youth community but had succeeded only in providing tents, food, and sanitary facilities to a group of young people with little interest in social change.

Still, I learned a lot from this battle. Fighting back really did work. My experiences at Wachea also helped me to appreciate that there were real class differences in Canada, too. In a way, I understood the campers' anger at us. We had education and could rely on our families should we run into trouble. Even though we were choosing to be poor, it was our choice, not a condition imposed on us by social circumstances. This realization spurred me to find a new way to battle the inequality that I saw. I started looking for another political route.

LIKE MOST SIXTIES RADICALS, I believed that the revolutionary transformation of society required systemic change. So in 1971, I began studying Marxism, eventually joining the Revolutionary Marxist Group (RMG).

Marxism made the world I saw make sense. It wasn't just the extreme poverty I witnessed on my travels, it was also the brutality of government authorities against anyone who opposed the war in Vietnam, the extreme oppression of Black Americans during the civil rights movement, and the Trudeau government's response to the October Crisis. Marx argued that because the capitalist ruling class had gained their wealth through violence, they would never give it up without violence. Therefore a violent revolution led by the working class would be the instrument of its destruction. Marx called the transitional society that would follow a "dictatorship of the proletariat," which would lead to a peaceful Communist society. Class would no longer be a defining factor; each person would contribute according to their abilities, and each would receive according to their needs. Stalin's and Mao's interpretations of Marxism resulted in the creation of strong states based on proletarian interests, but used violence or mass imprisonment as a way to stop dissent. After Lenin's death in 1924, Stalin took over the leadership of the Bolshevik party and went so far as to imprison and murder those who disagreed with him even within the ranks of his own party. The Russian theorist and politician Leon Trotsky was the first to argue against this authoritarianism. He warned that party bureaucrats were taking the place of the capitalists, instead of building an alternative society where workers and peasants controlled their own communities and lives. Trotsky was vilified by the Communist regimes in Russia and China, but we loved him.

In the United States radical groups like the Black Panthers and the Young Lords, a Latino group like the Panthers, were linking U.S. imperialism to racism at home. The Weathermen, the radical group that emerged from Students for a Democratic Society, were so convinced that a revolution was coming that they tried to instigate it by bombing government offices. The FLQ had similar politics, linking their struggle to national liberation struggles around the world. Starting from the Mau Mau Uprising in Kenya and the Algerian Revolution, almost all the anti-colonial national liberation struggles used forms of guerrilla violence. Most of the people involved in revolutionary politics in Canada did not think violence in the present context was useful, but we believed a violent revolution would ultimately be necessary because the bourgeoisie would inevitably defend their power with arms.

The other factor for me was the leadership. The RMG, and the Red Circle before it, had powerful women leaders. Jackie Larkin had been the Ottawa organizer for the Waffle, a radical wing of the New Democratic Party, and managed to convince them to lend her to the Abortion Caravan, the first national action of the women's movement. Jackie was small, lithe, and tough, while still being charming and loving. Deirdre Gallagher came from a trade union family and already had quite a bit of experience in the labour movement. She seemed softer than Jackie but she, too, was tough and powerful. Deirdre was one of the few in our group who had a child. In those days, we weren't interested in having children and considered it a diversion from the movement. She says that she got almost no support for her parenting. Varda Burstyn was tiny but mighty. She was, and probably still is, one of the smartest people I have ever met. I knew Varda because she was a friend of my brother Alvin in high school. All three of them were powerful women, great speakers, tough feminists, and very sexy. They played a leading role in the Waffle and in the RMG. They were all friends with each other and I, too, became friends with them. Even today it's unusual to find a political group in which women play such a major role, but in the 1970s it was unique and irresistible to me. The three women, and in particular Varda, played a key role in establishing International Women's Day (IWD) as a yearly march in Toronto that would bring together and make visible diverse feminist groups.

About a year after I joined, the RMG wanted to start a chapter in Vancouver and asked if I would be willing to go. It seemed like an exciting opportunity, so I took off with my boyfriend Will Offley and another friend, Heather MacNeil. When we arrived, we were living in a collective house in Vancouver's east end with Steve Penner and Gary Crystall. Gary was what we would have called a "contact," someone identified as a potential recruit. Later, Gary went on to found the Vancouver Folk Festival, but he was already interested in music and had lived in Chile for a while before returning to Vancouver.

Since Gary had lived in Chile, pressuring the Canadian government to allow Chilean refugees to come to Canada became a major activity. In late fall of 1973 we occupied the Vancouver passport office in protest. It was the second time I got arrested in Vancouver. The first time was a month before. Will, Gary, a fellow comrade named Heather Prittie, and I were at a party. The RMG was involved in picket support for the mostly immigrant workers who were striking for a first contract at Artistic Woodwork, a picture frame manufacturer. The company called the police to escort scabs over the line and it became one of the most violent strikes of the time.

A couple of our comrades had been beaten up and we were pretty upset about it. We didn't realize that Artistic Woodwork had an office in Vancouver until we were getting into Heather's car and Gary noticed a big display window saying ARTISTIC WOODWORK.

"Let's break it," he said.

"Great idea," Will responded.

Heather and I didn't think so, but that was irrelevant.

Gary told Heather to kill the lights, drop them off, and circle the block so they could jump in the car just as the window was shattering. The moment they started throwing the rocks, a squad car drove through the nearest intersection. I can still hear the thunderous crash of glass shattering into a million pieces. The cops were at our car in an instant.

"Judy, you talk to them," Gary said.

I figured if I could talk my way out of being searched for drugs at the Israeli border, this should be a breeze.

The cops told all of us to get out of the car.

"What's the problem, officer?" I asked.

"Didn't you hear that window break, miss?"

"Yes, of course, but we don't know what happened."

I kept chatting to him, calmly and respectfully. My ability to dissociate from fear and anxiety was serving me well until he said, "Open the trunk."

Inside the trunk were piles of the newly printed *Old Moles,* the RMG newspaper. On the cover was a picture of the picket line at Artistic Woodwork with the headline "Smash Artistic Woodwork."

We were all arrested but only Gary and Will were charged. Gary had a record so Will took the rap. He got two years' probation, which was a lot more than we expected.

I left Vancouver almost a year later, mostly because I couldn't take the rain. What I didn't realize then was that I was suffering from another depression.

When I arrived in Toronto, I was elected to RMG's political committee, a group of about seven people who met weekly to decide on the direction of the organization. I was leadership now, which meant I was even more devoted to the political work. My day job was working at City Hall as a clerk. It was a boring and depressing job. When I heard from a friend that the Canadian Hearing Society was looking for a secretary in Information Services, I jumped at the chance. Within a year Denis Morrice promoted me to be Director of Information Services at almost twice my starting salary. Even so I still considered it just my day job with politics being my real work.

The strange thing was that the only person from Vancouver I was missing was a man named Ken Theobald. Ken was a Maoist and most of the Maoists in Vancouver treated us Trotskyists like maggots. But Ken wasn't like that. He was a working-class guy and curious. I met him at a BC Federation of Labour convention and we started hanging out together. He came to my goodbye party, and much to my surprise the only image I had of leaving was of him. When I arrived in Toronto, I moved into a two-bedroom apartment on Sackville Street in Cabbagetown, then one of the cheapest neighbourhoods in the city. That summer, Ken stopped by on his way home to visit his parents in Windsor. He called to see if he could stay with me. I was surprised but agreed.

We talked most of the night and then he held my hand. One thing led to another and he stayed the night. When I told Varda about it, she suggested that we take the weekend, go to her parents' house (they were out of town), and spend some concentrated time together. I guess we fell in love.

After a few months of a long-distance relationship, he moved in with me. Ken is a rather unassuming man. Very attractive, quiet with a sense of emotional depth. After my relationship with Roger ended I was never again attracted to alpha males and preferred men who were not aggressive.

The first couple of years together were good. For some inexplicable reason, even my father liked Ken. We went to my parents' place for dinner every Friday night, which had been my habit ever since I moved back to Toronto. Ken liked my parents and his presence seemed to have a calming influence on the family. He thought my father was hilarious and there was nothing Jack liked better than an attentive audience.

After some study, Ken joined RMG, even though he never felt very comfortable among all the high-powered middle-class intellectuals and was not nearly as engaged in the work as I was. But life was good. We both had good jobs, decent incomes, a healthy sex life, and a stable home life.

About a year after Ken moved in, I heard from Roger for the first time in years. He was back from England and claimed he was off the booze. He asked if he could visit. I asked Ken to stay in the apartment, just in case things became difficult with Roger.

I was shocked at how old Roger looked when I opened the door. Of course I knew he was thirteen years older than me, but when I was twenty-one he was still a relatively young man. Now he was well into middle age and much the worse for wear. He kissed me chastely on the lips and was overly happy to see me. He was a perfect gentleman and as loving as ever. But seeing him did not bring back those old feelings. In fact, I was a little anxious. I didn't feel a close connection to him anymore—I had buried my feelings for him, along with all of the other feelings I didn't want to deal with.

"You look great, Judy. You know, of all the women I've been with in my life, you were the most special to me."

"Thanks, Roger," I said, surprised and maybe a little suspicious. "But you know I was just a kid then."

"No, you were no kid. You were smart, savvy, sexy, tough. You were not a kid."

Just then, Ken walked into the kitchen and I introduced them. Ken made it clear that I was with him. Roger could see there was love between us.

He stayed about half an hour and then said goodbye. *That was painless*, I thought.

Then the notes started to arrive. There was one a day for about a week. I couldn't really understand his scrawling handwriting, but what I could make out was very disturbing. At the end of the week, he called. He was drunk, very drunk.

"Seeing you with someone else was too painful for me, Judy," Roger said. "I want you back."

"I'm with someone else now, Roger."

"I know, I know."

"Please stop sending me notes. They're kind of upsetting."

I don't remember what else he said but he didn't call again and stopped sending the notes. The next time I saw Roger was on the street, almost twenty years later. He was walking like a zombie. I was in the middle of therapy and had just become president of the National Action Committee on the Status of Women (NAC). He told me that he was studying pottery at George Brown College, permanently off the booze, and had been diagnosed with bipolar disorder. The zombie walk was a side effect of the drugs he was taking. I took his number but when I finally called him, about a year later, it was out of order. I never saw or heard from him again.

AS PART OF MY political practice with the RMG, I became involved in other organizations. I joined the Committee Against Racism and Political Repression, founded by Black radicals, including Akua Benjamin, who remains a friend to this day. Its objective was to stop the deportation of Rosie Douglas, who had just gotten out of jail for participating in the most important Canadian anti-racist action to date, a 1969 sit-in at Concordia University that resulted in the destruction of the computer centre. Rosie always claimed that an *agent provocateur* trashed the computers, but he was convicted of mischief and got an eighteen-month sentence. After he got out of jail, he continued to organize against racism, often in coalition with Indigenous activists. The government wanted to get rid of this charismatic Black leader. We organized across the country but failed to stop the deportation, which finally happened in 1976. Later, Rosie became the prime minister of Dominica.

I also joined the Committee to Defend the Self-Determination of Quebec. This committee was formed sometime after the Parti Québécois victory in 1976 and continued until after the 1980 referendum. The committee was an alliance between the Trotskyists who had always defended Quebec's right to self-determination and whose Quebec wing supported independence and other independent leftists. Given the massive polarization around the 1980 referendum, we got very little attention in English Canada, but it was good experience to stand up for a very unpopular political position in the middle of what sometimes seemed like a war.

Because the RMG believed it was training the leadership of a not-too-distant future revolution, I learned a lot of skills. I learned not to be discouraged if things didn't immediately work out. "The long view," we called it. I was also trained as a public speaker. In 1975, when Philip Agee, the former CIA agent who left the agency over the United States' secret wars in Latin America, came to Canada to promote his book *Inside the Company*, the RMG asked me to chair the large public meeting that we sponsored. I was nervous and one of the male leaders told me, "Don't worry, Judy. If you say it with confidence, everyone will believe you." A secret of the patriarchy that I learned well.

By then faction fights were erupting within the organization. It was a sign of the times that political debates were very polarized. You took a position and held on to it for dear life. My need to play a leadership role brought intense pressure, leading me to bury my feelings more and more. There was also pressure on RMG from Fourth International, the international Trotskyist organization to which we belonged, to fuse with the League for Socialist Action (LSA), an older and more male-dominated left-wing political group. Many of them had been through 1950s McCarthyism, when Senator Joseph McCarthy led a series of investigations against Communists and Communist sympathizers in the United States, and didn't like our sex, drugs, and rock 'n' roll free and easy ways, or our combination of New Left and Trotskyist politics. We thought the LSA were squares and didn't like their politics either. I think they agreed to the fusion with RMG because they figured they could defeat our politics, pick off some of the leadership, and get rid of the rest. And that is exactly what happened.

After a big debate, which I helped to lead with Steve Penner, we pulled off a fusion of the two political groups in the autumn of 1977 and formed the Revolutionary Workers League (RWL).

IT WAS AFTER the fusion that things really started deteriorating for me. I was spending more and more time and energy on the new organization and less on my relationship with Ken. We were fighting more, not just about politics but about everything. What began as a loving, close relationship soon became distant and argumentative. I began feeling more anger and less compassion for those I disagreed with, both inside and outside the RWL.

About a year after the fusion, I agreed to go on staff for the organization and move to Montreal. Ken didn't want to go to Montreal, but at this point he was not a priority and neither was my job at CHS. I was so immersed in political activism I didn't think about anything else. I became extremely isolated in Montreal, working mostly in French, living in a city where I no longer related to my old *McGill Daily* friends, most of whom thought I was crazy for being a Trotskyist. My good friend Steve Penner was there, though, and he was as obsessed with "the movement," as we called it, as I was.

On top of that, the fusion wasn't working and a major part of the old RMG wanted a split after a difference emerged, mostly around RWL's decision to "make a turn to industry," meaning that we would all get industrial jobs to be closer to the workers who we thought would be the driving force of a socialist revolution. Moving middle-class university graduates into factory jobs seemed foolish to many RMG members.

Steve and I couldn't understand why people wanted a split. We had worked so hard to unite the two organizations. I remember a tense leadership meeting in Montreal after members of the former RMG within the group had left. It became clear that I was now in an organization where I didn't like anyone. Almost everyone I cared about had left the Revolutionary Workers League that I had worked so hard to help form. It wasn't so much that I questioned the new organization's ability to bring about change without my RMG comrades; it was that I felt too isolated and abandoned to fight alone.

I left one meeting with Steve and Léon, a Quebec comrade, and started to cry. Steve put his arm around me and said, "It's okay, Judy. Don't worry about it. If you can't handle it, that's okay. Léon and I can do it."

Something in me hardened. Suddenly, the tears were gone and so was any feeling of grief. There was no fucking way I was going to let two men take over because I couldn't handle it. I would never give up my leadership that way. Failure to do what was necessary was not an option. Once again I completely detached from my emotions, but this was a turning point.

I believe that in this moment I created a new adult personality. She was tough and cold, and she was the last of the alters to emerge in therapy. From that point on I buried all my feelings except anger. But that didn't last long either.

Ten

DOWN THE RABBIT HOLE

SOON AFTER THE SPLIT of the RWL, I decided to go off staff, return to Toronto, and make the turn to industry.

The first sign of my deterioration was physical. Problems with my digestion turned into serious pain in my abdomen. A specialist admitted me to hospital because of my history with amoebic dysentery following my trip to India. He believed my liver might have been compromised. I went through a series of tests that felt like torture. Every test made the pain worse. I was admitted the day before John Lennon died in December 1980. I remember crying when I heard the news. I had always loved John Lennon.

"What are you crying about?" the nurse said. "Don't be ridiculous."

They also gave me painkillers that made me hallucinate. When I told them that I was hallucinating, they just put up the bars on the sides of the bed, which panicked me even more. I called Kristi, my massage therapist, and she talked me down. Then the young woman in the bed next to me started to cry.

"What's wrong?" I asked

"I don't know," she whimpered. "I started feeling pain in my stomach and it's getting worse."

I buzzed the nurse.

"What's wrong?" she asked when she came in.

"The woman in the next bed is in pain."

The nurse checked her and then told me not to worry.

I tried to sleep but woke up when the woman started screaming.

The nurses came in and talked to her like she was a child.

"Stop screaming. It's nothing to worry about." But she wouldn't stop. They gave her some medication but it didn't help.

I looked at the woman and saw she was in terrible distress. Even under the influence of painkillers, I was able to react to the crisis. I got out of my bed and went to the nursing station.

"She's in trouble, call a doctor," I insisted.

"Don't worry," said the nurse. "She's taken Valium, that will help. She's just a hysteric." Later, I found out that she was anorexic.

I knew something was very wrong. I started roaming the halls, calling out for a doctor. A doctor came with me to the room and after a brief examination rushed the woman into surgery. They had left a hole in her esophagus, so the Valium had gone into her body cavity. She could have died of septicemia. I, on the other hand, only had irritable bowel syndrome, but it was a sign of things to come.

SOON AFTER I RECOVERED, in January 1981, I got a job at McDonnell Douglas, an aircraft factory just outside of Toronto. Ken had moved to Montreal to be with me a couple of months before we both decided to move back to Toronto. Now we were living in a flat above a store on College near Bathurst. I was still a part of the Revolutionary Workers League, and many of our comrades were getting jobs in industry.

Finally, I was living my political beliefs. There was a sense of class-consciousness and even solidarity on the plant floor. The entry-level job at McDonnell Douglas was deburring using a drill with tough sandpaper to clean up the airplane wings. The work wasn't bad until I woke up one morning and found my right hand was paralyzed.

I ran hot water on my hand and the feeling came back.

"I woke up this morning and my hand was paralyzed, completely paralyzed," I told my workmate. In those days, we didn't know about repetitive stress injury.

"Oh yeah, happens to all of us."

"How long does it last?"

"We all have it. It never goes away."

"You're kidding, right?"

"No. It doesn't go away. No big deal. Just run hot water on it."

"Why don't you complain about it?" I said. He laughed.

A few weeks later, the manager asked if I wanted to transfer to the wing department to do chemical milling.

"A girl was transferred over there a few months ago and she's doing pretty good," he said. "So we thought we'd try you."

Fuck, I can't believe the chauvinism in this place, I thought.

It was a reclassification, a semi-skilled job. I think it paid $2 an hour more, $13 an hour if memory serves, and that was a lot of money in those days. I was happy. The work was more interesting. Standing at a drafting table, we would trace a stencil onto the metal wing. A crane would dip the wing into acid, leaving the necessary indentations from the stencil. There were two problems: the bath consisted mostly of sulphuric acid and nobody wore the protective suits because they complained they were too hot. Now and then, when the crane would go off balance, the guys would put a wooden block on the end of the crane. Sometimes the block would drop into the acid and if you didn't move fast enough, you'd get acid splashed in your face.

"No problem," my workmates would tell me when I objected. "The sink is right there, just wash it off."

"What if it gets in my eyes?"

"You wear glasses. No problem."

Damn, I thought. *I'm the girl and if I complain they're going to be even more pissed off that I'm here.*

The other problem was the shift work. This job had three shifts and the midnight shift was killing me. I had trouble sleeping during the day; my digestion was affected, and I felt tired all the time. And the danger of acid burns increased when everyone was so exhausted. Driving home from work at 7 a.m., I had to put my head out the window so I wouldn't fall asleep. My workmates taught me that trick, too.

Finally my six-month probation was over and I could get involved in the union. Soon after I got off probation, I went to a union meeting where there would be a vote to strike. I've always been a powerful speaker so when I spoke from the floor in favour of a strike, my intervention got noticed not only by my fellow workers but by the boss. Guys started to drop by my workstation to talk to me about workplace issues. Then management started harassing every person who came to talk to me. Soon no one was coming and I became quite isolated. Then one day at lunch break, I found a threatening note in my lunch box. It was made out of letters clipped from a tabloid newspaper and said, "Fuck Off and Die, Commie Bitch." It had to be from one of my workmates.

I started to feel quite ill. My doctor said she thought I was allergic to the acid bath and instructed me in no uncertain terms to quit my job. Today I think my illness might have been due to the stress, the isolation, the threat, and the repression of the emotions that came with them. I listened to the doctor and quit. Going home that day, I felt such liberation, like I was driving a convertible with the top down, my hair flowing in the wind.

The next morning I woke up and couldn't move. When Ken got home from work, I was still in bed. I hadn't eaten or slept. It was like I had fallen into a deep dark hole and I just didn't have the energy to climb out of it or even ask for help. I felt a weight inside my chest, pressing down on my feelings, my energy, my desire, myself. I had lost interest in everything. I didn't care about anything or anyone. For an activist that was worse than death.

Then there was the anxiety. Everything made me anxious. I couldn't eat either. In my last month in Montreal, my sister-in-law Glenna told me that she had lost twenty pounds in a couple of months on the Atkins diet, a high-protein diet popular at the time. She said it was easy so I tried it. I lost thirty pounds in a couple of months. The move from Montreal, starting work in a factory, a failing relationship, the loss of most of my friends at the RWL, and losing thirty pounds led to unbearable stress, but I didn't give it much currency. I could handle anything. I always had.

This time, however, it was too much. This time I couldn't work, I couldn't concentrate, I couldn't do much of anything.

It's hard to describe what it feels like to be clinically depressed because in essence, it is an absence of feeling. The most famous metaphor is Sylvia Plath's bell jar. By this time, I had totally buried my feelings. Ken and I were still together, but I was distant. I started seeing my massage therapist, Kristi Magraw, again. She believed that a lot of emotional pain was held in the body and that massage could release it. This is common knowledge now, but back then she was a pioneer. She recently told me that when I first came to see her my body was very numb as if it were totally covered in armour.

When I went to my doctor, she diagnosed me with clinical depression and wrote a prescription for pre-Prozac antidepressant pills. The first day I took them, I had a hallucination that ice water was racing through my veins. I immediately stopped taking the drugs. I knew I couldn't just lie in bed all day, so after a couple of weeks I called my old boss at the Canadian Hearing Society, Denis Morrice,

Grandma Schutter and baby Judy.

Judy with her younger brother Alvin.

Judy, age five.

Leonard, Judy, and Alvin.

Left to right: Lenny, Grandpa, Ruth, Jack, Grandma.

Jack and Ruth on the dance floor.

Judy, age twelve.

Judy delivering her first speech at Alvin's bar mitzvah with Lenny to her left.

Ruth and Judy, age twenty-two.

Judy at twenty-five with Leonard, Glenna, and a friend.

Judy during her hippie days.

Judy with Denis Morrice, Executive Director of the Canadian Hearing
Society.

September 1983: Dr. Henry Morgentaler telling reporters in Toronto
that he plans to resume abortions at his downtown clinic. Judy is on
Morgentaler's right and Norma Scarborough is on his left. (Photo by
David Cooper/Toronto Star via Getty Images)

January 29, 1988: The front page of the *Globe and Mail* after the Supreme Court ruled the previous day that the abortion law violated Section 7 of the Charter of Rights and Freedoms, infringing upon a woman's right to "life, liberty, and security of the person."

Dr. Henry Morgentaler with his arms raised in a V for victory sign. (CP Images)

July 30, 1990: Judy, as President of NAC, speaking at a peace camp in the town of Oka, in support of the Mohawk of Kanesatake.

Wed Feb 21, 1990

This is my first attempt to contact
my alters thru writing so who wants
a turn

ME I AM SICK TO DEATH
OF YOU AND YOUR WAYS
I FEEL THAT YOU WILL NEVER
HAVE FUN NEVER BE ANY
GOOD AND NEVER TRY
ANY HARDER TYBE ANY
GOOD NO MATTER HOW
MUCH TIME THEY GIVE YOU
IT WILL RUN OUT AND
I WILL BE WAIT IN
FOREVER AND I AM
VERY FRUSTRATED IN TH
ALL OF THIS SO WHY

Pages from Judy's journal.

Thur Feb 22

too many men here too many men here
no here no here so like hangover not
secret fuck off hangover so like too many
men watch out look out notans here
anywhere damn trouble not from much

(large scribble drawing)

fearsome fearful fat not here
your not here gone

CAN'T YOU BE HAPPIER
OF SOMETHING BECAUSE
I AM REALLY TIRED OF
ALWAYS HAVING TO PROTECT
YOU FROM EVERYTHING

Sophie?
~~Simon~~

with known persons / less than seven
years are not heard from until you
and we also have something to say but with
known persons more than seven years
keep talking all the space really louder &
wanting they would go away so we could come out
I play & not also tried all the time

Amy

PLSS PLSS

I feel so sick perhaps I
am sick or perhaps someone is
sick near I am so sick

Tues Feb 27

My name is not Poonched
My name is Phoebe not
Posha but Phoebe and
I am not as stupid
as you think I am so
there and why don't
you let me come out
more I know it

you are hopeless
but also lies
all you
life a die
u lie a lie
lie lie

telling him that I was ill and couldn't keep working in the factory. He offered me a contract to set up a sign language interpreter service. I took it.

To give you an idea of how changed I was, most of my co-workers described me as shy and quiet. Most days, I was incapable of working; I'd just stare out the window. Our office was in a beautiful Victorian mansion in the Annex, the downtown residential neighbourhood near the University of Toronto. My desk was at the front window on the ground floor looking out onto a peaceful tree-lined residential street. One day a week, I'd feel able to work and got enough done to satisfy the job requirements.

In February 1982, I went on leave from the RWL. One day, Joan Campana, a comrade who had recently won a million dollars in the lottery, asked me to have lunch with her. She was so shocked by the change in me that she offered to pay for a trip to Cuba that the Socialist Workers Party, our U.S. counterpart, was organizing. I accepted her generous offer, figuring a week in the sun would fix me up, not to mention a visit to the only society that was close to our vision of what socialism might look like. Despite the limits on democratic expression, I appreciated how they prioritized children, education, and equality for women and Black people. But even though I loved Cuba, its wonderful people, and the beach, the trip didn't help. When I got back, I decided maybe I did need a therapist. My doctor had suggested I go into therapy when she diagnosed me with depression, but at the time I refused. I didn't believe in therapy.

Mark Smith, who had been a youth worker for the Addiction Research Foundation when I was working for the Trailer in Yorkville, had become a psychologist and I went to see him. I remember our first meeting. He worked out of a small office in Rosedale. Mark is tall, classically handsome, well groomed, and fit. Not my type at all. But it was easy to trust him and we had quite a bit in common politically.

"I don't want to talk about my childhood or any of that crap," I said to him. "I don't believe in it. I just want to talk about why I can't do my work." My main concern was returning to political activism. "Can you help?"

"We can't do a lot while you're depressed," he answered. "The depression will run its course and then we can do the work of finding out what's causing it."

"How long will that take?" I asked, thinking, *When that happens I won't need therapy anymore.*

"Generally, a depression like this will last nine months. In the meantime, we can talk about what is happening to you today," he said. "What are you worrying about—Judy Rebick becoming a dishrag?" He laughed, but that was exactly what I was worried about. I was limp, just like a dishrag. I had lost my energy, I had lost my motivation, I had lost my interest in life, and I had lost my sexual desire. What else was left?

The truth was that I rarely felt much during those days. In some ways, I had turned into my father. All my feelings were channelled into anger. My sense of humour was gone, too. One of the things I remember about those early days of therapy was that Mark told me I presented like a man: I was worried about my political work, not about my relationships. Women were usually more concerned about

134

relationships. Things with Ken were going badly, but that just wasn't important to me.

Many of those therapy sessions were devoted to what I now think of as a reconstruction of my personality. I had driven myself into the ground. The Judy Rebick that Mark had known ten years before had disappeared. Now, with his help, I was digging myself out, piece by piece.

Ken wasn't very sympathetic. "You have a good job, a relationship, a place to live, a good relationship with your family. What have you got to be depressed about?" he would ask, thinking it was helpful. We didn't know much about mental illness in those days. He himself was suffering from agoraphobia and I didn't have much sympathy either.

The worst moment between us was when we were having dinner one night in February in our new apartment in High Park.

"Today's my birthday," Ken said quietly. "You forgot."

I was devastated. I never forgot birthdays; they were so important to me. I realized I was still really depressed. I wasn't getting better.

Ken and I had an open relationship. "Breaking down monogamy" was part of the cultural experimentation of the late 1960s and early 1970s. Comrades were very serious about not becoming possessive or taking ownership of their significant others. They struggled with their jealousy, but challenging monogamy was an important part of their politics. For me it was no big deal. I never felt jealous. Since Roger had been my first major relationship, open relationships seemed normal to me. I had my political work and Ken had the odd affair with other women, which had never bothered me until I became depressed. I felt so insecure, so anxious, that I asked him not to get involved with anyone else until I felt better. But there was little left of what had once been between us. Ken got involved with a woman he was working with, and he wouldn't end things with her. So we broke up. I don't know if I threw him out or if he decided to leave, but I always believed he abandoned me. That wasn't true: he had hung in for months trying to make it work.

Ken was a packrat who kept piles of newspapers, which he had always planned to clip for research, in the second bedroom. Seeing the empty room after he moved out made me realize that I had just lost the one man who had stuck with me through thick and thin. The pain was so great that it broke through the armour that the depression had spread over my feelings. For the first time since the split in the RWL, I cried. But this time, I couldn't stop. I had to get out of the apartment. I called Leonard for help. He and his new wife, Andrée, came over to get me. They took me to their house, where I cried for hours.

When it was over, the depression had finally lifted.

THE SUMMER AFTER I emerged from the clinical depression, my mother visited from Fort Lauderdale, where she and my father had been living since he retired in 1977. I saw them in Florida every winter and they came to Toronto every summer. My father thought he would continue working in Florida as a salesman, but his body had another idea. Soon after moving there, he had surgery to unblock his arteries. Even more serious, the following year he suffered a brain aneurysm that required surgery. I went down to help out. My mother was more upset than I had ever seen her.

"He's not himself," she told me when I arrived. "I don't know if he'll ever be the same."

We went straight to the hospital.

"Hi Dad," I said, leaning down to kiss him on the cheek. He laughed and started singing like a happy little boy. It was almost as if he were celebrating my arrival.

My mother was extremely worried, despite the doctor's assurances that he would return to his old self once his brain started to heal. My reaction was different. I found him quite delightful and wouldn't have minded if he retained this cheery, childish demeanour. It lasted about two days and never returned.

It was the summer of 1982. I was still in therapy with Mark. When he heard about my parents' visit, he suggested I talk to them about the depression to see if we could identify a history or a reason in my childhood for such a serious illness. I invited my mother to my apartment for a private talk. I had moved to a lovely old building on Vaughan Road, and I suggested she come over to see my apartment, as I knew my father wouldn't be interested. After showing her around, I offered her a coffee.

"It's a lovely place, Judy."

The last time she had visited my home was when she and my father came to my bachelor apartment in Montreal in 1967, my last year at McGill. I was living in a tiny room up five flights of stairs that had a bar instead of a kitchen, with a hot plate and a fridge. I slept on a single bed that doubled as a couch and washed the dishes in the bathtub because the bar sink was so small. I think it cost me $50 a month. My father was upset when he saw the place, but given that he was broke and couldn't contribute to my rent he kept his mouth shut.

Vaughan Road was a palace by comparison. My mother sat on the couch and I pulled up a chair to sit opposite her with my back to the TV. I served her coffee and she lit up a cigarette. I had quit smoking several years before because Ken had chronic bronchitis. In 1982, no one asked permission to smoke inside, especially not my mother.

"Mom, I want to ask you about something. You know I've been depressed." I don't remember talking to her about the depression, but she knew about it.

"Yes, dear. I'm glad to hear you're feeling better."

"Thanks. I was just wondering if you have any idea of why I would be depressed. Depression is often hereditary. Did anyone in the family suffer from depression? Did anything happen to me in childhood that could explain it?"

She hesitated for a moment and then said, "You know, we've never been close." Being open didn't come easily to my mother. It was a big effort for her to say this.

I didn't think our relationship was so distant, but somehow I couldn't say that to her. I was a devoted daughter and in her way she was a committed mother. All my friends loved my mother. She was so kind and thoughtful. Sometimes I thought about how she was never that kind and thoughtful to me, but I figured it was just the usual mother-daughter friction. My mother was the good parent.

"You cut yourself off from me when you were five years old," she said sadly.

"What?"

"It's true." She sighed. "And it never changed. There's always been a distance between us."

"But Ma, why didn't you do something?" I asked, pleading to know, to understand. "I was only five years old. Why didn't you do something about it? Get help. Get advice. Find out what was wrong."

"Well, we didn't know about things like that in those days. What could I do?"

That was her answer to everything. Let's move on. No sense in dwelling on the past.

In preparing me for the conversation with my mother, Mark had identified that I had become emotionally independent from my parents at the age of five and he told me that I should ask my mother what she remembered about that time. My mother didn't know why and I didn't know why either.

WE STARTED THERAPY in earnest then. I don't remember much about the sessions but Mark taught me some important lessons. He showed me how I saw the world in black and white when really there was quite a bit of grey. He explained that a crisis is often followed by a period of wandering. Most cultures have stories of wandering after a crisis, for example Moses and Jesus who both had long periods of wandering in the desert. Mark thought that after therapy I would no longer be a revolutionary activist. His view was that I would have gained too much perspective to be a radical, but I think that was his projection. It actually made me a more effective activist. Being able to see multiple perspectives on my own life allowed me to better understand my opponents, even Right to Lifers who would soon be my opponents. It has been an invaluable skill.

But Mark wasn't entirely wrong. Soon after my depression began to lift, I started going to RWL meetings. At one meeting, Barry, a particularly ornery and somewhat obnoxious comrade, was being expelled from the organization.

Barry defended himself and then the chair asked for speakers. No one but me put their hand up.

"As you know," I said, "I don't agree with Barry, but one of the reasons I joined this movement is because we believe in the right of tendency. I don't see that Barry has done anything to threaten our movement; he just disagrees with this campaign. He might be more obnoxious about it than most comrades, but in essence his views and actions are no different than many other currents that have existed over the years. I think expelling him would threaten our principles as a movement."

They voted to expel him. To me, democracy was always the most important characteristic of Trotskyism. Unlike other Marxists, the Trotskyist movement allowed the right of tendency, which meant that those who had minority opinions in the group could organize support for their views and even set up a sub-group to push for those ideas. This was central to our notion of democracy. If the RWL was going to stop supporting the right of minority opinion, then it wasn't the kind of group I wanted to be part of after all. I looked around the room: almost everyone was from the old LSA. Barry was one of the younger members of the RMG, so maybe they were purging us. During the time I was on leave, Steve's beliefs had aligned more and more with LSA's thinking. I was the odd man out, so to speak, so I decided to quit.

The next day, I went to a meeting called by a group of women who were providing birth control counselling in the city. They explained how difficult access to abortion was under the law passed in 1969. That law permitted abortions for the first time, but they had to be done in a hospital with the approval of three doctors who formed a Therapeutic Abortion Committee (TAC). Access was very limited. The birth control counsellors spent most of their days on the phone, waiting to get an answer from a hospital that performed abortions. Most would never get through. The group wanted to set up an illegal clinic in Toronto to challenge the abortion law, like Dr. Henry Morgentaler had done in Montreal. Someone nominated me for the coordinating committee.

I accepted.

Eleven

GET UP, STAND UP

I WAS NOT READY to wander in the desert just yet. Instead, I jumped into the abortion battle, a struggle that was as all encompassing as the RWL.

Moving from a far-left group into the women's movement was not as much of a cultural shift as you might think. I, along with other RMG women, had been involved in the International Women's Day (IWD) Committee since its founding in 1978.

The 1980s was the height of the women's movement in Canada. In addition to the battle on choice, women were fighting for pay equity, affordable and accessible child care, and gender equality under the constitution. There was already a network of rape crisis centres and shelters providing services to women and advocating for better laws and more awareness of male violence against women. Young women had established co-operative daycare centres on campuses across the country and were working to get government support. We had the struggles of the seventies under our belts, having learned a lot about organizing and lobbying. And there were more women in professional jobs, which provided both a financial base and a certain access to power that we hadn't had during the previous decade, but women were still struggling for equality.

I knew some of the women in what became the Ontario Coalition for Abortion Clinics, who were active in IWD. Many of them considered themselves socialist feminists. At the beginning OCAC was a coalition of these socialist feminists with the more moderate women from the Canadian Association for Repeal of the Abortion Law (CARAL) and radical feminists who saw men as the enemy. So there were lots of differences within the organization, but the most difficult thing for me to deal with was the radical feminists who were hostile to male doctors even though we couldn't find a female doctor who was willing to work at an illegal clinic at first. I didn't see men as the enemy and was particularly supportive of trying to convince Dr. Henry Morgentaler to open the clinic in Toronto.

The radical feminists were uncomfortable with our supporting a Morgentaler clinic. They wanted a women's clinic that feminists would control. But when the first physician recommended by Dr. Morgentaler didn't work out, we all agreed that it was better to have a Morgentaler clinic than no clinic at all.

Our first indication of public support for the clinic was at a rally we held in the winter of 1983 at an auditorium in downtown Toronto. Dr. Morgentaler was the featured speaker and I was the MC. People were lined up around the block to get into the room, which had a thousand-person capacity. We knew there would be Right to Lifers in the audience, so I was ready.

When Dr. Morgentaler began to speak, they started chanting, "Murderer! Murderer!"

I asked them to stop, but when they wouldn't I called out to the crowd, "What do we want?"

"Choice!" they responded.

"When do we want it?"

"Now!"

I got the crowd chanting "Choice! Now! Choice! Now!" drowning out the opposition and raising everyone's spirit. The chant was used at future demonstrations and rallies. The hecklers were removed by ushers.

At the end of the rally, Dr. Morgentaler gave me a big hug. I was not much of a hugger but I knew he was so I tolerated it.

"Judy, would you be willing to be the spokesperson for the clinic? I need someone in Toronto to do the job and I like your energy," he said.

"I'll need to discuss it with OCAC, but sounds good," I replied.

It was the first time I had met Dr. Morgentaler.

THE PRO-CHOICE BATTLE gave me renewed energy and a powerful sense of purpose. But looking back, there were signs that I had still not completed the necessary emotional work post-depression. I had done much valuable work reconstructing my personality with Mark, but part of me was still buried. Between my political activism and my job, I had little time to think about how I was feeling. I just barrelled through the days, avoiding any introspection, but something always stopped me.

That summer I suffered a near-fatal accident. I was riding my bike on my way to Harbourfront for one of the many meetings I attended to build support for the clinic. It was morning rush hour, and I was worried I was going to be late so I took Bathurst Street, which I usually avoided because of the steep hill and the TTC yards. I was rushing down the hill when my front wheel got stuck in the streetcar tracks. My body was thrown over the handlebars, and I came crashing down onto the road. We didn't wear helmets in those days, but luckily I had broken my fall with my hands. When I came to, I was surrounded by worried people, one of whom was the man whose car had stopped inches from my head. I had a terrible pain in my left wrist and my left side, so someone called an ambulance. When I got to the hospital, the doctor, who spent more time flirting with me than examining my injuries, said my wrist was broken. I told him my side hurt more than my wrist.

"It must be a muscle cramp," he responded.

That week I was scheduled to go to Oberlin College in Ohio, where the Socialist Workers Party was having a summer educational. Even though I had quit the RWL, I was still politically aligned with the group and kept in touch. The large campus was spread out across many miles. The pain in my side was gone, but I was still having trouble walking. Once I got home, I went to see my doctor. She touched my side and said, "Your ribs are broken, Judy." The X-ray showed the ribs were not only broken but had separated. As soon as I heard the diagnosis, the pain was unbearable and I had to stay in bed for a month to recover. It was a sign that I was still dissociative.

Fortunately Alvin and Glenna had rented a cottage with a beautiful beach on Georgian Bay, and they spent time taking care of me. But my obsessive running and dieting were sabotaged by the broken ribs. Ever since I had lost the thirty pounds, I became obsessed with watching my weight, dieting, and jogging about five kilometres a day. After the bike accident, all I could do, and all I did do, was eat. I gained all the weight back in one month. The post-depression therapy with Mark was putting me back in touch with my feelings, but I was still keeping so busy I could push my emotions away. Now that I couldn't do anything, I could not help but feel my emotions.

Just before it was time to go home, my parents came to visit from Florida. On the drive back to Guelph, I was still in a lot of pain, both physical and emotional. Alvin was driving, my father was in the front seat, and I was in the back. My parents hadn't seen me cry since I was a little girl and I didn't want them to see it now. I'm not sure if it was my father's presence in the car or the bumps on the road, but my ribs, which were still hurting, got a lot worse. The pain was excruciating, but I held it in as long as I was in the car with my father.

As soon as we arrived at Alvin and Glenna's house in Guelph, I asked if I could go up to their bedroom to rest. Once I lay down, the tears started to come. Crying turned to sobbing, sobbing turned to anguished weeping. Alvin heard me and rushed upstairs to see what was wrong.

"I'm in terrible pain," I whispered.

Before he could say anything, my mother appeared at the door. "Stop crying!" she yelled. "Stop crying! What are you crying about? Stop it!"

"Get out," Alvin said to her. "Go downstairs, you're not helping."

I think the look on my face made him realize that the weeping was not just from physical pain. He put his hand on my back.

"It's okay, you can cry as much as you need to. Ignore her. You know how she hates any kind of emotional display."

It wouldn't be the last time Alvin rescued me.

WHEN I GOT BACK to Toronto, I felt profoundly alone. Leonard had cut off his relationship with the family as part of his attempts to heal from our childhood, so his support was no longer available to me. My relationship with him was becoming more distant. He was also involved in a new therapeutic group. At his invitation, I attended one of the meetings and found it to be profoundly manipulative. But he was so committed I didn't feel I could express my true opinion. To be fair, I'm sure he felt pretty alienated from me during my Trotskyist days.

I didn't see him or his family very often anymore, so I plunged right back into my activism. On June 15, 1983, Toronto's first abortion clinic opened, and I stepped in front of the man who tried to stab Dr. Morgentaler with garden shears. It was a moment that changed my life, cementing my public image as a warrior, fighting for women's rights. It was also yet another warning sign that I was dissociative.

About a week after the opening, the chief of police announced that they had a complaint from a woman who claimed she had been forced to go through with an abortion at the clinic. The moment the news went public, the clinic received phone calls from the taxi driver who had driven the woman home and said she was fine until the cops stopped her; a nurse from the hospital emergency room who said the police had coached her; and someone from Immigration saying that she was an illegal immigrant and no doubt they threatened to deport her if she didn't file a complaint against Morgentaler. We had so much public support that they couldn't get away with lies and intimidation.

Then, three weeks after the clinic opened, Dr. Morgentaler and his colleague Dr. Robert Scott were arrested. Those three weeks were intense. Every day I would ride my bike from the Canadian Hearing Society to the clinic. The police were following patients home, trying to intimidate them, so OCAC organized what we called an "escort service." People would volunteer to take the patients home. The escort knew how to handle the police and what the patient's rights were. The escort service turned out to be a solid core of support for the clinic.

The day after the doctors were arrested, we held a big rally at Queen's Park. About five thousand protesters showed up. I was the MC and it was here that I really started to understand the power of public speaking. Through call-and-response chants, I could build the energy and enthusiasm of the crowd. In some ways, the pro-choice struggle was the perfect battleground: I could release my anger constructively by confronting a ferocious, sometimes violent, opponent in the anti-choice movement, yet I wasn't powerless as I had been in the face of my father's violence. I was empowered by the strength in the solidarity of the growing movement.

Death threats were common not only against Henry but also against Norma Scarborough, who was the spokesperson for CARAL, and myself. People used to call CHS, warning the receptionist that they would beat me up when I left the office. The worst incident was when a death threat had been posted to Norma's apartment door. Then there was the time when a man tried to throw me off a subway platform. Fortunately, I was taking tai chi and I took my stance so he couldn't move me. When the subway arrived, I ran.

I asked Henry how he coped with the constant threat of violence.

"Any of us could die at any time," he said. "We're doing what we believe in. There's nothing we can do about some crazy who might come out of nowhere and take a shot. We can't let that stop us from doing what we think is right."

We also received an incredible amount of support. One time I was on my bike passing a big truck when the driver yelled out the window, "Hey, you're the girl from the Clinic. Sam," he said to the guy next to him. "Look, it's the girl from the clinic." And then he gave me a thumbs-up.

Almost every time I went out for lunch or dinner with Henry, the servers would pay for the meals. From time to time when I was on the subway, people would give me money for Dr. Morgentaler and his defence fund.

"The courts are against us, the government is against us, the cops are against us," Henry once said. "But the people, Judy, the people are with us."

And so they were.

Twelve

THE CLINIC WILL STAY OPEN

ON OCTOBER 14, 1984, Dr. Morgentaler and his colleagues stood trial for performing abortions at the Toronto clinic. I remember only three things from the trial. First, the anti-Semitism. It so happened that Henry, his lawyer Morris Manning, and I—the three most visible people on the pro-choice side—were all Jewish. More than one cartoon exaggerated Morgentaler's Jewish features and another looked like something drawn up by the Nazis to mobilize hatred against the Jews. People would drive by the clinic and scream, "They only kill Christian babies in there."

The second thing I remember is that I was an unindicted co-conspirator, which means they were thinking about indicting me for conspiracy, however unlikely.

Finally, I remember Manning's closing argument to the jury: "Send a message to the Attorney General saying, 'Stop prosecuting doctors for helping women'...You can say we can't stand for this anymore. That we won't stand for this anymore."

We were all blown away by his moving and brilliant summary. No doubt Henry's testimony also had a tremendous impact on the jury of six women and six men. After a hushed courtroom heard his history of survival in the Nazi death camps, he said, "I decided that helping people could never be a crime."

The jury deliberated for only six hours and delivered the verdict: not guilty.

THE VICTORY WAS short-lived. On December 4, 1984, Ontario attorney general Roy McMurtry announced the government would appeal the jury's verdict. The next day, Henry announced the Toronto clinic would re-open on January 7, 1985. McMurtry said it was up to the Toronto police whether to re-charge the doctors. At this point, Dr. Morgentaler had asked me to step down as spokesperson for the clinic. He felt I was too abrasive and too radical. He wanted the clinic to be known as a peaceful place, a medical facility. I agreed. Instead, I would use my media profile to become the spokesperson for OCAC. Carolyn Egan, Norma Scarborough, and I still met regularly with Henry and his lawyer to discuss strategy. We tried to co-ordinate legal, financial, and street activities. Manning understood that public support was essential to influence the judges. We often disagreed but we continued to work together.

The anti-abortion groups decided that they would demonstrate in front of the clinic every day so that patients were forced to cross a picket line of aggressive people often carrying horrible pictures. To protect the patients, we put out a call for women and men to meet the patients, walk them into the clinic, and escort them home if they wished. Hundreds of people responded, and over the next few years formed a cadre of support for the clinic and the movement. We also won a contested resolution at the Ontario Federation of Labour convention, which meant that we had not only the official support of the labour movement but also a lot help to get through the difficult moments of the struggle.

On February 12, 1985, Toronto Archbishop Cardinal Carter sent a pastoral letter to 196 parishes, calling on them to mobilize with the Right to Life demonstrators in an attempt to shut down the clinic. OCAC called for a demonstration at Queen's Park on February 22, to protest their attempts to shut down the clinic. CARAL, the more moderate pro-choice group, was against calling a counter-demonstration, thinking we wouldn't be able to out-mobilize the Catholic Church. Up until then our biggest demonstration had consisted of five thousand supporters. The Catholic Church had mobilized more than that over four days. We were getting worried.

I will never forget the day of that Queen's Park protest. Standing on the steps of the Legislature, I was overwhelmed by the thousands upon thousands of people streaming out of the subway. People had come from all over southern Ontario. By our count around fifteen thousand people had shown up to the demonstration. This, I believe, was the turning point in the struggle.

On October 1, 1985, the Ontario Court of Appeal ruled

against Morgentaler, set aside the jury's verdict, and called for a new trial. As a matter of course, the Supreme Court agreed to hear the arguments.

Despite the Appeal Court decision, Henry kept the clinic open and OCAC continued to organize support through rallies, public speaking, media work, and debates.

Shortly thereafter, OCAC had a major dispute with Morris Manning, Henry's lawyer. At the time, Manning was defending a couple of companies who were trying to break unions in high-profile cases. Not only did we worry it might undermine some of our union support but many of us objected in principle. We had asked Henry to fire Morris but he refused. I was very upset about it. We decided that I would go to Montreal with two female labour leaders to try to persuade him.

We met Henry in his hotel room. He argued that lawyers were hired hands and it didn't matter who else they defended.

"What if Manning defended James Keegstra [an Alberta neo-Nazi]? Would you get rid of him then?" I said.

"It's not the same thing," Henry insisted.

"It is for me," I replied.

I'm surprised he didn't ask me to leave. The other two women were horrified that I would say such a thing.

Henry asked to talk to me privately and we went down to the hotel bar. "I know you're doing this because you believe it's the right thing for the movement, Judy. I hope you realize that I'm insisting on keeping Morris for the same reason. The most important thing is that it doesn't interfere with our friendship."

I was genuinely moved. Until that moment, I hadn't realized that our friendship was important to him. I knew my role in the movement was important to him, but I didn't know that he cared about me. I also realized then that I cared about him. On some level, he helped me understand the importance of personal relationships in overcoming such a difficult struggle. More than that, he was a model of courage with an open heart, whereas I was courageous because I couldn't feel fear.

Henry didn't fire Morris, but as a compromise he did criticize Morris publicly for taking that case. In retrospect I think he was right and I was wrong.

IT WOULD TAKE another four years for the Supreme Court to rule on abortion. During those four years I had resigned as spokesperson for OCAC and run as a candidate for the Ontario New Democratic Party. Because I was no longer the spokesperson for OCAC, I didn't travel to Ottawa with Henry to hear the Supreme Court decision. I stayed in Toronto. OCAC called on supporters to wait outside the clinic. As soon as the decision came down, Carolyn Egan, the founder of OCAC, would call us from Ottawa.

As we were waiting, a reporter tapped me on the shoulder and said, "Just heard from our guy in Ottawa. The Supreme Court struck down the abortion law based on a woman's right to security of the person."

I wasn't sure what to do. I didn't believe her. We thought we might win, but not on a matter of principle. Security of the person was, in essence, our primary argument for overturning the current law: a woman had a right to control her own body. A few minutes later, we got the word. The journalist had been correct.

On January 28, 1988, the Supreme Court ruled that the abortion law violated Section 7 of the Charter of Rights and Freedoms, infringing upon a woman's right to "life, liberty, and security of the person." Chief Justice Brian Dickson wrote: "Forcing a woman, by threat of criminal sanction, to carry a fetus to term unless she meets certain criteria unrelated to her own priorities and aspirations, is a profound interference with a woman's body and thus an infringement of security of the person."

It was a total victory.

We were jubilant. The reporters wanted to interview me, but I declined because I was no longer a spokesperson for OCAC or the clinic. But they persisted.

"How do you feel, Judy?" one of them yelled.

"I feel great!" I said, jumping up in the air. "I feel great!"

The clip appeared on almost every television newscast, running just after Dr. Morgentaler raised the V for Victory sign as he walked out of the courtroom with Norma Scarborough and Carolyn Egan.

A few years later, I met Chief Justice Brian Dickson, who had penned the majority court decision. He told me of all the things he had done in his life, the Morgentaler decision was what he was most proud of.

FOR MOST OF those years, the intense waves of activism kept my head above water. I had finished with therapy midway through this period, but two things emerged close to the end of my treatment that have stayed with me.

At one particular session, an angry male voice emerged from deep inside me. I didn't seem to be controlling it but I could hear it. Mark explained it was a dissociated ego state, quite common in people who are burying a part of themselves. But soon The Voice emerged again and I had to talk to it. Now I believe it was one of my alter personalities.

For weeks and even months The Voice would speak to me. I could control whether it spoke out loud but I could not control when it spoke to me. The Voice was the cynic who thought every gesture of kindness was motivated by some kind of evil intent. "Oh yeah, what does he want?" The Voice told me I couldn't trust anyone and had to rely only on myself. Mark, my therapist, told me to listen to the caution, which was often justified, but not to generalize it; I was capable of knowing who to trust and who not to trust.

The Voice was worried about Jeremiah, a man I had started seeing about a year after Ken left. He was handsome, charismatic, and intelligent. I didn't usually get involved with dominant men, but he was persistent and he was living with someone else so I didn't have to worry about getting too serious. I figured he had an open relationship, but when I found out he had been lying to his partner, I ended it. He moved to Victoria soon after, but we kept in touch.

About a year later, I went to Vancouver, probably for a speaking engagement, and we got together. We began an on-again, off-again long-distance relationship that lasted for years.

Whenever I had contact with Jeremiah, The Voice would

break into my consciousness, warning me that if I got more involved I would be terribly humiliated. I wrote in my journal:

I felt deep in my chest an anger so terrible it was like a lion's growl and it was anger at whoever treated me badly enough to make me feel that expressing love subjects you to base humiliation.

I ended my relationship with Jeremiah, not from the humiliation The Voice had warned me about, but from disappointment.

After three years of therapy, Mark and I both agreed that I had made great progress. My sense of humour had returned, I was slowly but surely getting in touch with feelings like sadness, disappointment, love, even moments of happiness. Just as important, I started to become more conscious of my feelings. Paying attention to them meant I could let them go.

And then came the second thing that stayed with me: on my last day of therapy I was lying on Mark's couch and a memory came to me like a dream. I was a little girl, maybe six or seven years old, and a man was touching me in a sexual way. The flashback lasted a couple of seconds. I didn't recognize the man, but it was clear that I was the little girl.

"What's wrong?" Mark asked, noting a change in my demeanour.

I didn't want to tell him what I had seen. I was functioning and feeling good about my rising public profile, and I didn't want to continue with therapy.

"Nothing," I responded. "It's nothing."

IV

COME TOGETHER

1989–1992

Thirteen

SOMETHING'S HAPPENING HERE

IT IS OBVIOUS as I write about my life in the 1980s that my activism diverted me from paying much attention to the turmoil that was rising to my consciousness. The endless challenges kept me from looking at the memories that openly threatened me from time to time. Total memory loss is quite common in childhood sexual abuse. Studies find that 19 to 28 percent of survivors have no memory of the abuse for decades after. After the depression lifted, the memories started to emerge but I wasn't yet ready to face them. I had done enough therapy to be fully functional, at least in the area of work, and that's what I wanted. I was an angry person but I was able to use that anger in the pro-choice struggle, a fight with a real enemy that was trying to destroy me and the lives of so many women. Fighting back was healing for me; winning even more so.

It wasn't until the fall of 1989 and Barbara Dodd, the deaf woman who fought against her boyfriend's injunction to stop her from getting an abortion, that the memories were let loose.

After a couple of sessions with psychologist Marcia Weiner, the memories started to emerge more clearly. I remembered my father was taking a shower. Lenny was sleeping in the bed across from mine. Sometimes I didn't even wake up when he was taking his shower, but this day I was awake.

He was standing by my bed. He didn't usually do that. His bathrobe was open and I could see his penis. It was big, much bigger than Lenny's. It scared me so I turned away.

"Look at me, Judy," he whispered.

"I don't want to."

"Don't be scared, *Maydey* [little girl]. It's all right."

He patted me on my back, encouraging me to turn over. When I did he took my hand and put it on his penis.

"No, Daddy, don't," I said, pulling my hand back. "I don't like it." I felt scared. I pulled the covers over my head. I was cold. "Stop it, Daddy. I don't like it, I don't like it," I said, my voice getting louder.

"Shh, we don't want to wake up Mommy, do we?" he said. But I still protested. He went back to his room, leaving me alone. On another day he tried again. "You want to help Daddy feel good, don't you?"

Finally, I did what he asked.

Piecing together the timeline, I figured the abuse started when I was four or five — the same age my mother had said I was when I became distant. It was also around the time when we left my grandmother's basement. Lenny would have been at school. My mother wasn't working and would have probably been busy with baby Alvin.

I spent a lot of time alone with my grandmother. I helped her cook and clean. She would sit at the sink and I would stand on a chair next to her to reach the dish rack. As I wiped the dishes dry, she chatted to me in Yiddish. She didn't speak much English, but her love came to me like the light through the front windows. There wasn't much love in the basement.

When company arrived, my father would lift her out of her wheelchair into an armchair, but I wasn't strong enough to do that. My job was to help her with her walker. With me next to her for support, she practised walking in the living room.

My father often got home in the middle of the afternoon. He would stand at the bottom of the stairs and call me:

"Daddy's home, *Maydey*. Are you up there?"

I went to the top of the stairs.

"I'm busy, Daddy. I'm helping Grandma."

Mostly he accepted this response, but this one time he insisted. Grandma told me to go.

"Come down here, Judy. Come and sit on Daddy's lap. Oh, you're so pretty, such a pretty little girl who loves her Daddy."

"No, I'm not pretty. I'm not. I don't want to come down. I'm staying here. I won't come."

Grandma was getting angry now, insisting that I go downstairs to the basement.

"Daddy makes me touch him, Grandma, and I don't want to. Please make him stop." Instead of helping, she got even angrier.

165

"*Shmutz* [dirt]," she said, and hit me on the ear. I felt like I'd been hit with a sledgehammer. I still feel pain in that ear sometimes. "Don't say those things! It's dirty!" Grandma had never hit me before. I wanted to tell her, *I don't wanna do dirty things. I try not to, really I try, but I can't help it. I'm sorry, Grandma. It's not my fault.* But I was too shocked to say anything. I just hung my head and slowly went downstairs.

That was the first time I told someone that my father was sexually abusing me, and the last time until forty years later when I recovered the memory in Marcia's office. It was as if that slap from my grandmother sealed the knowledge of abuse into a part of my brain that I couldn't access. I think this must have also been the moment that I started to dissociate. If my grandmother wouldn't help me, no one would. I had to help myself.

After a few sessions with Marcia, each one revealing more memories, a thought came to me when I was alone in my living room: *I am a bad person. Everyone thinks I'm a good person, but now it will come out how bad I am.* My adult self knew that whatever had happened wasn't my fault, but I started feeling that the Judy everyone knew was not real. The real person was not a good person. I would be exposed. *I better kill myself now so no one finds out.* It seemed so rational, so sensible. I told Marcia how I was feeling.

"I don't think I can go through this, Marcia. I can't stand feeling so helpless. All my life I've felt powerful and in control. Now I see all that was a lie."

"It wasn't a lie, Judy. It was part of your reality. You hid the feelings of helplessness and shame so that you could be powerful in your life. That's how you survived. Now you're ready to face them. That's why you're here. That's why your memories have revealed themselves. You're ready and I can help you get through it."

"I don't think so, Marcia. I really don't think so."

"What are you saying, Judy?"

"I'm thinking about suicide. It's not that I'm depressed. I just can't see myself through this. I don't know who I am anymore. I feel like I'm falling apart, literally. There's no centre. There is no me. The person I thought I was, who is that? I don't know anymore."

"It's true that you've kept a part of yourself hidden until now. You've buried your memories so that you could live the life you wanted to live. I'm not going to tell you it'll be easy, but you're a fighter. I've seen women with much less strength go through this process. Not only will you survive, you'll be a fuller person — more yourself, not less. I know it doesn't feel that way now but I have seen many women go through similar experiences."

"I don't think I can do it, Marcia. I don't think I can."

"Okay, let's try something. I have an agreement here." She pulled out a piece of paper from her file. "It says you won't try to kill yourself before our next appointment. I'm asking you to sign this agreement, just for a week. It's a way for both of us to make sure you survive until we see each other again."

She held the paper out for me to take. As I looked down at the floor, my stomach tightened. I shook my head no. "I can't, Marcia. I can't sign it."

For some reason I wasn't willing to lie to Marcia the way I sometimes did with Mark.

Her brow furrowed. She frowned and after a pause said, "You know that my ethics require me to report this. If I do, you might be hospitalized."

"Please don't do that. Being hospitalized is the worst thing I can imagine right now, but I just can't sign that agreement. I know I have to be honest with you if this is going to work. How about if I take it home and think about signing it?"

"Okay, Judy. I'm going to trust that you'll be here next week. Please don't let me down."

I'm lucky she didn't commit me. I'm also lucky that I had a good job and a cheap apartment, so I could afford private therapy. If I had to rely on the public health care system, I'm not sure I would have been able to stay out of the hospital.

It wasn't the agreement that stopped me from killing myself; it was my friend Gord Cleveland.

"Think of the children," he said. He meant his daughters, but it made me think about my nieces, Kael and Terra, and how it would affect them. At sixteen, Kael was the eldest. Terra was fourteen, and Gord's kids, Tara and Julia, were thirteen and eleven. All of them would have been devastated by my death.

The next week I signed Marcia's agreement.

It was September 1989 when I began the journey into my childhood, discovering hidden memories and extraordinary defences both fantastic and terrible.

AS SIMON SAID, there were others. Every session, more and more of the personalities emerged, different ages, different genders. After a few months, I drew a chart with Simon, HIM, and Sophie, who were older children, on one level and Mary, Pricilla, Lila, and Lobo, who were clearly little children, on another. Marcia called them "alters." They protected me, the core of me, from becoming even more damaged.

I thought about moments in the past that could have been experiences of dissociation. One occurred in the early 1970s when I came back to Toronto after travelling around the world. I was living in a commune on Cowan Avenue in Parkdale with mostly men, one of whom was Gary Penner, Steve's brother. He was younger than I was and a musician. He became a good friend whom I connected with again in the 1980s. Soon after we reconnected, I suggested that we have sex. Gary responded, "We tried that before, Judy, and it didn't work out too well."

"Oh yeah," I responded but I had no memory of it. That troubled me at the time, but like everything else I just forgot about it. We remained friends and later I asked him about that night, admitting that I didn't remember having a sexual experience with him.

"We went to see the Downchild Blues Band play at Grossman's," he began. I remembered that. Gary used to play with them and I was astonished when they invited him onstage.

"It was a great night and when we got home, we started kissing in a way we had never kissed before. Then we went upstairs to my room." I didn't remember the kissing but I did remember going upstairs with him and opening the door... and then nothing. There was no memory. That is the nature of dissociation. There's not even a glimmer of memory, just a concrete wall. The wall separated me not only from the abuse but from other memories that threatened the alters, even if my conscious self did not feel threatened. What I realized was that having sex with a close friend reminded them of the sexual abuse. Even though I was unaware of their existence until therapy with Marcia, they did seem to be affecting my memory and to some degree my behaviour.

Multiple personality disorder, or what is now called dissociative identity disorder, is an extreme version of normal dissociation. "Dissociation is the essence of trauma," wrote Bessel van der Kolk, in his brilliant book on trauma *The Body Keeps the Score*. We all dissociate sometimes.

In my case, my ability to dissociate, which continued without my knowledge into middle age, permitted me tremendous courage even in the face of physical threats like the Morgentaler attack; endurance and an uncanny ability to work long hours, almost never resting despite how tired I was; and detachment, usually emotional detachment from implications of relationship and events. If anything got too painful, I just stopped thinking about it; I sometimes forgot that it ever happened. Only occasionally did I feel anything strongly other than anger. I never missed anyone or anything after my grandma died in 1955.

The American Psychiatric Association defines it this way:

Dissociative identity disorder is associated with overwhelming experiences, traumatic events and/or abuse that occurred in childhood. Dissociative identity disorder was previously referred to as multiple personality disorder.

Symptoms of dissociative identity disorder (criteria for diagnosis) include:

The existence of two or more distinct identities (or "personality states"). The distinct identities are accompanied by changes in behavior, memory and thinking. The signs and symptoms may be observed by others or reported by the individual.

Ongoing gaps in memory about everyday events, personal information and/or past traumatic events.

The symptoms cause significant distress or problems in social, occupational or other areas of functioning.

The purpose of therapy now, Marcia explained, would be to integrate the personalities so I wouldn't split off anymore. Therapy with Mark had put me back in touch with my feelings, to a point. Now I would meet and assemble all the fragmented parts of myself.

As to multiple personalities, all I knew was from seeing the movie *The Three Faces of Eve*. The movie about Eve White, a mousy, middle-aged housewife who went into therapy because she was acting strangely, had had an impact on me, along with everyone else in the late 1950s when we didn't know anything about mental illness. In therapy, her other personality, Eve Black, who was sexy, outgoing, and adventurous, emerged flirting with the doctor and sashaying around the office. Her husband called it her "moods," but the doctor realized there was something deeper at work.

My experience wasn't anything like that. I was not aware of behaving differently or even being particularly moody. The only thing I noticed was that I had huge blanks in my memory. Important parts of my childhood were not accessible to me. I remembered summer camp but very little about what happened at home. Over time, I realized that I had few memories of being at home with my father in Toronto, where my family had moved when I was ten. I had memories of being there alone, with my brothers, with a babysitter, but almost never with my father. I also forgot some important moments in my adult life. *I have too much to think about*, I would tell myself. *Lots of people can't remember things.*

The day of Simon's first appearance, he continued talking to me after we left Marcia's office. His voice wasn't like my own interior voice. His words appeared in my mind with a distinct quality — stronger, more forceful, addressing me as though I were a different person.

"Judy," he said. "We need you to stop communicating with Jack. We're all afraid of him and I think you might freak out if you see him or talk to him."

This seemed reasonable to me. Since beginning therapy with Marcia, I could not envision having an ordinary conversation with my father. Luckily, my parents were living in Florida. I called them once a week and usually talked to my mother, but it was always possible that my father might answer the phone. Simon said I had to cut off all contact.

"I don't think I can control the others if they hear Jack's voice," he explained. "No Jack."

"Okay," I agreed.

Cutting off contact with Jack made sense to me, but it

meant cutting off contact with my mother, too. That was hard. I was not ready to tell her what I was going through. I usually visited my parents in February but it had only been a couple of months since the memories emerged, so I knew it was too soon to see them. I asked Alvin, whom I had told about the abuse and the personalities over Christmas, to explain that I would be out of touch for a while. We agreed he would say I was going through some tough psychological stuff and needed to be on my own. My mother's tendency toward denial meant she wouldn't ask too many questions. It was a lot to ask of him, but I didn't see an alternative. I thought I would be out of touch for a few weeks, but it turned out to be for two years.

I just couldn't face Jack.

Fourteen

THE POLITICAL BECOMES THE PERSONAL

I FUNCTIONED BY COMPARTMENTALIZING. In therapy, I was willing to explore my hidden mind, but in my life I was still avoiding the memories. So much so, that as an active feminist for more than a decade, I had never gotten involved in issues that addressed violence against women; I hadn't even attended the Take Back the Night marches. Subconsciously, I feared they would bring up my own history of abuse.

All that changed on December 6, 1989. It is a day I will never forget. I was driving home from work when I heard the news on the radio: a gunman was shooting students at the École Polytechnique, an engineering school affiliated with the Université de Montréal. I slowed down and turned up the volume. Who was he killing? How many? Why?

I parked my car in front of my apartment and listened to the radio. Then I heard it: the man had separated the men

175

from the women, then shot twenty-eight students, killing fourteen women. While he was on his rampage, he said, "You're all a bunch of feminists and I hate feminists."

I could hardly breathe. A man had targeted the female students at a school where the vast majority were male. He killed them because he believed that feminists had ruined his life. He killed them because they were training for a man's job. He killed them because they were women.

I felt sick. I ran up to my apartment. The minute I got in I turned on the radio and the TV. I started feeling cold, really cold. I looked at the thermostat; it was at 21 degrees. The apartment wasn't cold. I was cold. A deep sorrow started to build in my belly. It grew and spread until I started to cry; the cry became a sob and the sob became a scream. I ran into the bedroom to get a pillow to stifle my screams.

Violence against women was epidemic but it wasn't until December 6, 1989, that the veil covering misogyny was lifted through this act of fury and hatred. The media were saying this was the act of a madman but most feminists recognized that rage. We had been talking about it for decades. We knew that it was an extreme act of misogyny we had spent our lives fighting. It was a profound public moment that had a deep impact on anyone who had ever experienced male violence.

I was only just beginning to understand how my father's rage and abuse had affected my life. The depth of grief I felt at the massacre was also personal grief. My father had not taken my life, but he had taken my innocence, my ability to love and be loved. He had taken my memory, my history. Up until that moment, my wounds were private. I had never consciously connected them to my politics. But now I was starting to make that link.

I called a friend to find out if there was a vigil or a rally. I needed to be with other women. A spontaneous memorial was planned for the next day. When I arrived at the location I saw about a hundred women bundled up in winter coats, quietly talking in front of *Crucified Woman*, a statue at the University of Toronto's Emmanuel College. It was late afternoon on a cold grey day. I hardly knew anyone. The first person I saw was Marilou McPhedran, a feminist lawyer whom I had debated recently on constitutional issues. Her usual confidence and energy were gone. It seemed as if the muscles in her face had collapsed. She was grief-stricken. I put my arms around her, not knowing what else to do. Neither one of us had ever cried in public. We came from the generation that believed tears showed weakness and we were strong women.

We didn't have a megaphone or a mic, so we gathered in circles around the *Crucified Woman*. There were a few men there, but it was the women I remember, their heads down, eyes lowered, soaked in sadness, still in shock. Some women were crying. Then someone began singing Holly Near's "Singing for Our Lives." We were grieving together as women, as feminists, as mothers, as sisters.

I'm pretty sure Marilou said a few words, or someone did, but mostly we talked about what had happened and what we were feeling. There were media asking questions and we answered in subdued voices, eyes downcast.

The week after the December 6 massacre, I was invited to speak at a rally on abortion rights in Montreal. Initially, the rally was to focus on Chantal Daigle, whose right to abortion case was going to the Supreme Court. But since it was only a week after the Montreal Massacre, it became a huge feminist memorial. Every well-known Quebec feminist—in the arts, the unions, politics, and the women's movement—was there. When I walked into the huge auditorium on Saint Denis Street, I was overwhelmed by the size of the crowd.

The women's movement in Quebec had been remarkably successful. They came from a highly patriarchal culture where women didn't even have the right to vote until 1940, twenty years after the rest of the country. The women in that room had fought for and won the same degree of equality as elsewhere in Canada in much less time. In one generation they went from the highest birth rate and the highest rate of weddings to the lowest. Women's status in society changed in a truly revolutionary way. Many feminists believed that the action of the assassin was part of a backlash against those dramatic changes.

However stunned we were in Toronto, it was much worse in Montreal. The hall was full, but it was quiet. In the bathroom, I ran into Françoise. She was a tough left-wing feminist who was never afraid to take a stand and speak her mind.

"He hated feminists." She was slumped over the sink trying to stop crying. "He hated us but he killed these young women. How do I deal with that?"

I nodded sympathetically.

"I feel guilty," she continued. "I know I shouldn't but I do."

"I understand, Françoise, but it isn't your fault they died. It's his fault."

"Yes, but one of the young women even said, 'We are not feminist.' Imagine! They blamed us, too."

"No, they didn't. She was just trying to save herself and the others."

That she felt guilty surprised me at first. But I found guilt in many of the women I talked to. He wanted to kill them, prominent feminists, but he couldn't get to them so he killed these innocent young women instead. Was it survivor guilt? No, it was another form of oppression. Blaming the victim is a component of oppression. It's part of patriarchy and sexism and it is part of colonialism and racism. What young women today call "rape culture" is full of this kind of shaming and blaming.

Radical feminists think all acts of violence against women are political. Violence against women exists to stop women from fighting back, from achieving equality both at a personal and at a societal level. There's little question that the École Polytechnique killer's act was political, just as there is little question that it was also personal, coming out of a rage against women taking his place in society. With the exception of a few prominent feminists, at the time no one in Quebec was willing to accept this explanation.

The events of December 6 reverberated through my body, my mind, and my memory. The pain of the original trauma of my father's abuse and anger, and of all the male violence I had shut out of my mind for years and years, flooded my consciousness. Today we call it a trigger, but back then I didn't really understand what was happening to me.

AFTER CHRISTMAS 1989, the different personalities started coming out more frequently. Marcia got each of them to agree that they wouldn't come out in public. It wasn't a problem with Simon, but some of them were small children with very little self-control.

"Hi, Marcia. I'm Lobo, and I can run fast, real fast, faster than anyone."

"Hi, Lobo. How old are you?"

"I'm five," he said, proudly holding up five fingers. Lobo was restless, jumping up and down and from side to side on the seat, standing and sitting, looking around. "I don't like it here, Marcia. Can I go out and play?" Lobo stood up and started for the door.

"Please sit down, Lobo. I'm sorry but you have to stay here with me. If you go out, you could get Judy into trouble. You wouldn't want to do that, would you?"

Lobo dropped his head. "No," he said in a small voice. "Can I go pee-pee?"

"Yes, the bathroom is right there."

Lobo jumped off the chair and ran to the bathroom where he tried to pee standing up, but that didn't work too well so I sat down and he disappeared. But not for long.

"We're starting to see the others now, Judy," Marcia explained. "It seems some of them are small children, so it might be difficult to control their behaviour. They want to protect you, that's why they exist. But they might come out so you have to be ready for that. Have you told anyone about the alters?"

"I told Alvin, but that's all. I don't think he really knew what I was talking about. There was enough to deal with, just trying to figure out how to continue his relationship with our parents," I said. "Alvin was shocked when I told him about the abuse, and now that I've told him about the personalities he thinks I'm a little crazy. It's not easy for him, trying to keep his relationship with me and with my parents. I don't want to put too much on him and I get the impression that he doesn't want to know too many details. He believes me and that's what's most important, isn't it?"

"Yes, of course. He's in Ottawa anyway. It's here you need some support. Decide which of your friends you trust with this kind of information and tell them. You might need their help."

"Okay," I responded, but I had no idea what she was talking about. I soon found out.

Marcia lived close to a Dairy Queen. Lobo was still around, as the alters often were just after therapy. He saw the Dairy Queen and came fully into my body and headed off. The Dairy Queen was about half a block north of Marcia's building on the edge of a cliff overlooking the Don River, a lovely location. Lobo skipped and ran along the sidewalk. I was hoping no one was watching a middle-aged woman skipping down the street with a big smile on her face. When we arrived, I noticed the woman behind the counter looking at me kind of strangely. I guessed that Lobo looked super excited to be at the Dairy Queen.

"What colour ice cream do you have?"

Now the woman knew something was wrong with this person. "Chocolate, vanilla, and strawberry," she said. Chocolate was Lobo's choice. At least in that he was like me. He sat on a nearby rock overlooking the Don Valley, kicking the rock and wolfing down the ice cream cone as any five-year-old would. I had sensitivity to soft ice cream. It had a strange metallic taste and made me nauseous and a little headachy and dizzy. But as I sat upon that rock I tasted what Lobo tasted, and it was delicious. There was no reaction to the ice cream as long as he was out.

When he was finished eating he disappeared, and my usual reaction to soft ice cream kicked in. I immediately got a headache and felt dizzy. It was the worst reaction I'd ever had. I found out later that alters can have not only different allergies from their host but even different medical conditions.

As I was learning, the mind is astonishing. At five years old, my mind had fragmented into different compartments to protect me from the terrible things my father was doing to me. I had created different personalities who employed a variety of tactics to try to stop him and to keep what he was doing to me from me. Once I started splitting into these different personalities, I no longer knew that my father was abusing me. For decades I had no memories of the abuse or any other events that the alter personalities considered dangerous.

I decided to tell my friends Sue Colley and Gord Cleveland, who I trusted and saw quite frequently. We'd known each other for a long time, and I needed friends who would guard my secret and give me support when I needed it. Sue and Gord fit the bill. Gord's mom was bipolar so they were used to dealing with mental illness. And since I spent part of the summer with them at their cottage in Muskoka, I knew they would notice if the alters came out.

I went to their house and told them. They were incredibly empathetic and supportive. I had already told them about the sexual abuse, which was a big shock. Telling them about the multiple personalities was easier because everyone reacted the same way to that. Curiosity. No one I told had any idea how to react to it. After, we turned on the television. Someone on TV said that everybody liked them and I said, "I wish someone liked me."

Sue and Gord both turned to me.

"Is that one of your personalities?" Sue asked.

"I don't know. I don't think so."

"It didn't sound anything like you."

"Maybe they can come out like that. I'm not sure."

Sue and Gord were a great support. Sue gave me a key, saying, "Any time you need help, feel free to come over. Wake us up if you need to. Whatever you need." I never took advantage of that generous offer but I was grateful for it.

Marcia and I agreed that the younger alters could come out with anyone who was aware of my condition. If the person knew I had multiple personalities, the personalities were allowed to come out. The problem was when an alter got scared and I hardly ever knew what caused that to happen. When one of them wanted to come out in public, I would feel nauseous. It was strange because I didn't feel that way when they came out in therapy or even in front of friends. Perhaps it was a warning sign so I could get away if I needed to. One time I was in a restaurant with a friend, and a friend of hers came in and joined us. For whatever reason, he scared one of the alters. I started to feel sick, excused myself, and left.

They usually didn't come out when I was working, but one day I was in a meeting with people from the pro-choice movement. We were discussing the idea of raising money for a full-page ad in the *Globe and Mail*, denouncing the new draft abortion law that Prime Minister Brian Mulroney was proposing. The women around the table had worked together for ten years in a fractious but still functional relationship. This time there was tension between me and some of the women over a recent dispute. I started feeling nauseous during the meeting, but I had to chair so I couldn't leave. Through silent thoughts, I tried to convince whatever alter was trying to come out to wait. Fortunately, the women around the table agreed on how to proceed and everyone was almost as anxious to get out of there as I was.

Once I got home, I used my journal to communicate with whatever alter had tried to come out. I had a feeling it was not one of the little ones.

"Who is there?" I wrote.

It was HIM.

HIM was the only alter without a name. The others referred to him as HIM. HIM was the only one who was angry at Simon. Some of the alters didn't know about Simon, but the ones who did loved him because he was taking care of them and me. HIM was angry at Simon because he came out to Marcia, whom he didn't trust, and HIM was always angry at me. Constant rage would be the best way to describe HIM. HIM never talked to Marcia; he just yelled. When HIM first came out, he tried to attack Marcia physically. That's when I learned that I had control over my body even when an alter was present. It took a lot of concentration, but I could stop

HIM from jumping Marcia and I did. Apparently HIM was willing to talk to me, if you could call it that, in the pages of my journal.

"You let them push you around just like you let Jack do those things to you. You haven't changed. You're weak. You should yell at them about what they did to you."

"It's not the same," I replied. "If I yell at them, it will just make it worse."

"Bullshit. Up yours. You know nothing. You're chicken, cluck, cluck. cluck. Let me at them and I'll show you how to do it."

The writing became illegible after that. That's when I realized that HIM sounded a lot like The Voice who had come out during therapy with Mark years earlier.

I was starting to get worried. In a couple of months, I was supposed to go to Gallaudet University in Washington, D.C., to participate in a week-long intensive sign language course at the only university for the deaf in the world. But with everything that was happening in my head, I wasn't sure I could handle it.

AROUND THIS TIME I made a list of the alters with descriptions of each as I understood them:

> *SIMON is a boy, very mature, calm, and thoughtful but not strong on feelings. He thinks that to get by in the world, you shouldn't feel things too strongly. He takes care of Judy and also the younger ones, Mary, and Pricilla. He keeps HIM in check so he doesn't hurt anyone. He is*

very worried about Judy now because she is upset so much of the time and he thinks she can't handle this level of feelings. He likes Judy, even loves her, but recognizes her weaknesses. He trusts Marcia, too. At first he was scared of her but not now. I am not sure how old Simon is. Marcia calls Simon the "guardian personality."

SOPHIE *is a girl and she is twelve years old. She wants to have fun and thinks Judy is a big fucking drag. She's really pissed off with therapy because it is taking all the fun out of life. She's the one who comes out when Judy is sexually attracted—the flirt, the game player—but Judy doesn't let that part of her out anymore so now she comes out more as the snarky part, a bit on the mean side. She likes Judy's friend Rob a lot but wishes Judy would seduce him instead of just talking to him. In fact, she's really getting pissed off with all this fucking talking and she is thinking about interfering more.*

HIM *is angry and mean and yells at Simon. He is furious that Simon has told Marcia so many secrets.* HIM *hates Judy for not fighting back and he never talks to her because* HIM *would probably get so mad he'd kill her, so Simon keeps them separate.* HIM *respects Simon though because Simon can take it and has held everything together for so long.* HIM *wishes Simon would take over.*

LOBO *is a little boy about five or six years old who can run faster than anyone and wants to run away.*

LILA *is a young woman of uncertain age with a Southern accent who is always smiling, rather seductive, and thinks if Judy had a more positive attitude to life, everything would be better. Lila is not Jewish.*

MARY *is a sweet playful child who skips and plays and doesn't know anything is wrong. She doesn't even know who Judy is.*

PRICILLA *is five years old and very scared.*

Fifteen

AND THEN THERE WERE NINE

IN THE WINTER OF 1990, two more personalities, Porsha and Trouble, emerged in therapy. Now there were nine. As soon as Porsha emerged, she started pounding my side. As far as I remembered I had never been into hurting myself, but there she was hitting herself with my fist. Oddly, I didn't feel anything.

"Where's Jack?"

"Jack is not here. He lives far away," Marcia responded.

"Don't talk to me like I'm a baby. I'm not a baby." She was angry at Marcia now and stopped hitting me.

"Who are you?"

"I'm Porsha. I've been around as long as Simon, you dope."

"Simon hasn't told me about you."

"That's 'cause he's stupid. He thinks he knows everything but he doesn't. I'm the one who stopped Jack, not him.

I'm the one who protects Judy, not him. He thinks he's so important. What does he do? Nothing. I'm the important one."

"Why don't you tell me about it."

"No way! I'm not telling you nothing. Why should I?"

"I'm trying to help Judy. Your telling me what happened helps her to remember. By remembering she'll start to feel better."

"What, are you kidding me? I know she feels better when she doesn't remember nothing. That's what's best for her."

"That's been true up until now, Porsha. But now Judy is stronger and she wants to know what happened so she can stop hiding from it." It would be a few more weeks before Porsha revealed her secrets to Marcia and me.

Porsha faded and Trouble came out. He was laughing.

"I'm Trouble, and I taught Judy to get sick," he said, putting his hands on his hips and lifting his head in a gesture of tremendous pride.

That was a real eye-opener. All my life, I had been sick off and on. In childhood, I got a lot of ear infections, not to mention every other illness going around. At sixteen, I suffered from a month-long depression. At eighteen, I had gallbladder surgery, rare for someone that age. In my therapy with Mark, I discovered that a lot of my physical illnesses had emotional sources. Kristi, my massage therapist, said that I somatized my emotional distress, meaning my body reflected my emotional problems.

Trouble revealed that getting sick was a defence. When I was sick my father never abused me, at least sexually. He just yelled at me. Once I vomited in my bed, and he dragged me into the bathroom and forced my head into the toilet. I've had a phobia about vomiting ever since. Throughout my life, illness was an escape. When everything became too much, I would get sick, mostly digestive illnesses. I thought I just wasn't taking care of myself, suffering from burnout, running myself ragged, but Trouble told me that it was another defence, like dissociation. Kristi would add that getting sick was the only way I could stop working so hard. What a mess!

Simon seemed kind of depressed at this point because he was losing control of all the alters (Lobo came out in that session, too) and that scared him. I was getting more and more worried. I considered whether I should cancel that trip to Washington, D.C., or if maybe it would be good for me to get away. I wasn't sure, but I always hated to admit defeat.

All I could do after that session was sleep. For weeks, I couldn't get enough sleep. I was feeling guilty about cutting off contact with my parents. I was also starting to notice a lot of fear. I thought that the personalities were making me afraid, but Marcia explained that as each personality emerged I would have access to the feelings they were keeping hidden from me, as well as the memories. Fear was the major one.

I would wake up early in the morning, at four or five, the hour of abuse, feeling terrified. The fear was like a glacier sitting on my chest, making it difficult to breathe and impossible to stay warm. I felt cold, so cold that it seemed I would never get warm. That's when I started taking hot baths in the morning to let go of the cold and with it the fear. When fear came on during the day, it was nausea that announced its arrival, and with it usually came an alter.

Somehow this fear didn't emerge when I faced danger or a threat in the real world. It was coming from deep inside of me and it was old, old fear, the fear of a child. The adult was still fearless.

February 1990 was the most intense month of activity for the alters. In an attempt to stop them from coming out everywhere, I decided to ask them to communicate with me in my journal. When I went back to those pages, I was amazed, mostly by the fact that all the handwriting looked different. Some of them signed their notes, some didn't. Some of the writing was incomprehensible.

February 21, 1990. This is my first attempt to contact my alters through writing, so who wants to take a turn?

ME I AM SICK TO DEATH OF YOU AND YOUR WAYS. I FEEL THAT YOU WILL NEVER HAVE FUN NEVER BE ANY GOOD AND NEVER TRY ANY HARDER TO BE ANY GOOD. NO MATTER HOW MUCH TIME THEY GIVE YOU IT WILL RUN OUT AND I WILL BE WANTING FOREVER AND I AM VERY FRUSTRATED WITH ALL OF THIS SO NO WAY. CAN'T YOU BE HAPPIER OR SOMETHING BECAUSE I AM REALLY TIRED OF ALWAYS HAVING TO PROTECT YOU. —SOPHIE

Little known persons of less than seven years are not being heard from enuf here and we also have something to say but little known persons of more than seven years keeping taking all the space and yelling louder. Wishing they would go away so we could come out and play and not be so tired all the time. —MARY

DESPITE THE CHAOS in my mind, I decided to attend the workshop at Gallaudet University, hoping the diversion would be good for all of us, me and the alters. As I had never been to Washington, D.C., I decided to stay downtown for one night, see the sights, and then go to the hotel near Gallaudet, a Holiday Inn that was in a poor, Black neighbourhood. I was fine until I tried to get a cab to take me to the Holiday Inn. The first driver refused to take me, after warning me against going there at all. When I finally arrived at the hotel, I went to push the door. When it didn't open, I pulled but it was still locked.

I tried again. Was the hotel closed? I was sure this was the right address. I could see someone had come into the lobby. I waved to get her attention, but she refused to open the door. Instead, she pointed to a sign that read: PLEASE SHOW YOUR PHOTO ID TO THE RECEPTION TO VALIDATE YOUR IDENTITY AS A HOTEL GUEST. The lobby was locked. I'd travelled around the world and I'd never been to a hotel where they locked the entrance to the lobby. I started to feel nauseous; the alters were getting restless. Maybe I'd made a mistake coming here.

Eventually, I got in but that night I had a lot of trouble sleeping. The nausea came and went, and later I had a strange dream. A blond girl was using sign language to interpret for me but she was talking at the same time. I told her to stop talking, but she wouldn't stop. She was grinning at me as if to say, *Up yours, I'll do what I want.* I argued with her, getting increasingly angry, and she just kept defying me. All at once I realized she wasn't an interpreter; she was an alter. I didn't know which one because

I didn't know what they looked like. When I woke up, I wrote in my journal:

Who is there?

Too many men here too many men here no like danger-
ous not safe fuck off dangerous no like too many men
watch out look out not safe here anywhere damn trouble
know from much. — PRICILLA

I had a headache and wondered if Trouble was causing it. I asked in the journal:

Trouble. Are you there? Who is there? What's going on?

There were two alters communicating with me. I am pretty sure one was Trouble.

You want to know what's going on fine ask but you don't
listen so fuck you . . . I told you not good here. Take a cab
not safe and you don't listen. — SOPHIE

Men too many men here don't like, very scary, you never
listen to us, always risk, don't want you alone too scared
too many men. — PRICILLA

I responded, *Yes, I did listen. I took a cab yesterday after-*
noon instead of the subway and I came right to my room.

194

*Because I made you feel bad you would have stayed out
and took the subway and everything so I made you feel
bad and that always works.* — TROUBLE

This was the first time any of the alters had tried to stop
me from doing what I needed to do. I was nervous. A little
nausea as a warning sign was one thing, but now I had a
terrible headache. I couldn't just stay in the hotel room. My
employer had paid for the course; how could I explain not
going? I had to work it out with Trouble. I was alone in the
hotel room so we had a conversation out loud.

"I'm the boss, do what I say or else I'll give you the worst
headache ever," Trouble said.

"But I *am* listening. I promise I'll take cabs from now
on and I'll find someone else in the hotel to walk to school
and back with me. The men are safe. They're not dangerous. They're students like me."

"You don't know if they're dangerous. Why are all the
doors locked if they're not dangerous?"

So it was the locked door that scared them.

"The doors are locked because there are a lot of robber-
ies around here, but I don't have anything valuable so you
don't have to worry. I promise. To tell you the truth, you're
scaring me more than the men."

That worked. No wonder I was tired all the time.

WHEN I GOT back to Toronto, I thought about writing my
mother a letter. She had just had some kind of stroke and
Alvin said she really wanted to talk to me. I figured I owed

her an explanation, but after consulting the alters I had second thoughts:

Is someone there who wants to talk about having contact with my mother?

Yes I do want to talk about it. I'm sick about it and can't believe you really want to see her. I am really sick about it really sick. Let her die who cares, just let her die from it. She deserves to die after what she did. I can't believe you really care about her at all ugh ugh ugh. —TROUBLE

I won't help you at all. I hate this stuff I hate you and your brother and I wish it would just stop. Oh you got my views now you shit fuck face. Who cares what she suffers after what she made us suffer. Who cares. —UNSIGNED

Simon here now. I feel rather differently about it. My view is that if your mother is willing to hear this, you should talk to her after all she was also a victim of Jack and maybe it would help you and I know you love her and would feel devastated if she died without seeing you or hearing from you so I think you should write that letter and see what happens.

NO, I WON'T LET THAT HAPPEN NO WAY CAN'T HAPPEN. TOO SCARY, TOO SCARY. —PORSHA

I didn't write the letter. My mother recovered from what was a ministroke.

While I was thinking about how I could survive the intense feelings and confusion produced by my therapy, Norma Scarborough asked me to have lunch with her. Norma was president of the Canadian Association for Repeal of the Abortion Law during the fight for the Morgentaler clinic in Toronto. In her sixties, a school secretary, and a mother who had lived in the suburbs, Norma was a comforting presence for our movement in the media. Her white hair, warm smile, and soft face belied a fierce determination in her commitment to the cause and to what she thought was right.

I hadn't seen Norma in a while. When I walked into the small coffee shop near the CHS office, I was very happy to see her.

"Judy, Doris Anderson and I were talking about who is going to take over as president of NAC this year."

The National Action Committee on the Status of Women was the most powerful women's group in Canada. NAC was a federation of more than five hundred women's groups from across Canada, ranging from the Conservative Party Women's Caucus to the Communist Party Women's Caucus to the Women's Temperance League to Vancouver Rape Relief, a radical anti-violence group. A new president was elected every year with a two-term limit. Doris Anderson, a pioneer feminist, had been president of NAC in the early 1980s.

During the pro-choice struggle, I was also advocating for employment equity as part of my job at CHS. In 1984, Justice Rosalie Abella produced a landmark report on employment equality. Instead of using the controversial American term "affirmative action," she coined the term "employment equity." More importantly she identified four "target" groups—women, visible minorities, people with disabilities, and Indigenous people—who faced higher levels of unemployment, underemployment, and wage inequality. On March 8, 1985, Flora MacDonald, the minister of employment and immigration in Mulroney's government and a true feminist, introduced a federal employment equity act in response to Abella's report.

People with disabilities, and agencies serving them, saw a real opportunity to fight for jobs in the context of the new law. My boss Denis Morrice asked me to co-chair a coalition of disabled people and agencies to lobby for employment equity in his stead. My role here was very different. I was a behind-the-scenes organizer, using my contacts and experience to create more impact.

My work on employment equity had soon led to my involvement with NAC. This was during the time of the free trade debate and NAC was playing a major role. Economist Marjorie Cohen had written an influential paper showing that the proposed free trade agreement with the United States would not only affect industrial jobs, but it would lower the standards of our social programs, which would have a negative impact on service jobs, most of which were held by women. Many of us felt inadequate when it came to debating free trade because of the focus on economics. Up until that point, feminist issues focused mainly on political and social inequality. Varda Burstyn proposed starting a Women Against Free Trade group in Toronto and I worked on that committee as well, learning more about the economics as we organized.

"We both agreed that you would be the perfect person," Norma continued. "We've consulted with quite a few women. They agree. With Mulroney in power we need a fighter and we need someone who's good in the media. You fit the bill. Plus I think women across the board trust you. You've travelled around the country, so everyone knows you. You've been involved with NAC committees over the last couple of years, so you know how the organization works."

"But I've never served on the NAC executive. Isn't there an heir apparent on the executive who wants to do it?"

"Not really. Everyone agrees you'd be the best person. If you want it, I'm pretty sure it's yours," Norma said firmly.

I agreed to run.

Sixteen

THROWING CAUTION TO THE WIND

THE OFFER TO BECOME president of NAC arrived at a moment when I needed to find a way through the chaos I was experiencing. I was feeling more and more helpless as I relived the abuse and tried to deal with the personalities. At the time the only book about childhood sexual abuse was *My Father's House* by Sylvia Fraser. Once she had recovered her memories, Fraser spent a lot of time alone, and in her words let herself go mad until she had worked through the trauma. I could never do that. My instinct told me that if I let myself fall into madness I would never get out of it. The personalities would take over and I would disappear. I needed to feel powerful in my life to survive.

In key moments of my life, I've known what I had to do. I get a feeling in my solar plexus, what some people call intuition or an inner voice. Despite my ability to dissociate from my feelings, I was always attuned to that intuition.

I didn't think about what I had to do; I just knew. What could make me feel more powerful than being president of the country's largest women's group?

Marcia was against it and so was my brother Alvin. Simon spoke to me through my journal on March 15:

I don't think you can handle this, Judy. I am very worried about things. You are sick and working too hard and now you're feeling like running for NAC, which I'm not sure is a good idea at all. I am worried that everything will collapse and you won't make it. I am very, very worried. I want you to think very carefully about this decision, very carefully because life is precious and you don't want to throw it away.

Up until this point I had listened to Simon. When he told me that the only way to protect my sanity was to cut off contact with my father, I did it. When he told me that I couldn't see Susan Swan because she scared too many of the alters, I did that, too. Susan was a very close friend who had helped me through a lot of hard times, but she was sometimes very invasive in her questioning. While it was a quality that I really appreciated, it scared some of the alters so I stopped seeing her for a time. But now I was certain that I couldn't survive the therapy without feeling powerful in my life and equally certain, as I always was, that I could handle it. I always felt better when I was active. The more work I did, whether in the women's movement or at my paid job, the better I felt. Working to change the world was like medicine to me. I needed to be engaged. I needed to help others. I couldn't survive if I just concentrated on myself.

Of course there were also political reasons for me to run. Conservative prime minister Brian Mulroney was moving the country to the right through the free trade agreement with the United States. NAC had played a major role in opposing the treaty, which would effectively weaken social programs. NAC had also opposed the Meech Lake Accord, a set of proposed amendments to the Constitution recognizing Quebec as a "distinct society," which was Mulroney's greatest priority because the province had not yet signed on to the Constitution, which had been repatriated from Britain in 1982. The Conservative government's response to NAC's opposition was to cut its funding and attempt to discredit the organization. Barbara McDougall, the minister responsible for the status of women in Mulroney's government, would say, "I belong to the YWCA because I want to swim and the YWCA is a member group of NAC, but NAC doesn't speak for me." If the organization wasn't able to show that it did indeed represent women, more funding cuts would come.

The Montreal Massacre had brought a whole new level of attention to issues of violence against women. The Mulroney government was trying to recriminalize abortion through Bill C-43. The Royal Commission on New Reproductive Technologies, which was looking at how to regulate new technologies like IVF, was beginning hearings. In some ways, the women's movement was at the height of its power, and I thought I could make a difference.

Mostly I kept my troubles a secret, but I did tell Alice de Wolff, NAC's executive director. I figured if anyone needed to know it was her. I told Alice in confidence about recovering from the abuse and even about the multiple personalities. She told me she wasn't worried because I was a strong, effective person. Later, she confessed that she didn't know anything about multiple personality disorder, and she might have been more worried if she had.

Just before the June 1990 NAC annual general meeting, in which I would be acclaimed president, the federal government cut $1.6 million from women's centres and shelters. In Newfoundland, women's groups occupied the secretary of state's offices for more than a week to oppose the cutbacks. The secretary of state was responsible for funding women's groups. The women mobilized tremendous support in the community with people delivering food and drink from around St. John's. NAC issued a supportive press release. Then one of the women from Newfoundland called and asked if I could help organize solidarity actions across the country through NAC's networks. As a lobby group, NAC was not accustomed to organizing street-level demonstrations, but the member groups mobilized into action.

The secretary of state was Gerry Weiner, so we had barbecue wiener roasts in front of his department's offices across the country. In Toronto we were dragged out by police after a few hours. John Crosbie, a much more powerful Conservative minister who was from Newfoundland, spoke out in Parliament, demanding that the government reverse the cuts. And they did. It was a tremendous victory for women's groups and set up my presidency as being a new wave of feminist activism.

Being NAC president brought a whole new level of public

attention to me. It's true that I was in the media a lot during the abortion struggle, but most people didn't know my name. I was the girl from the clinic or Morgentaler's spokesperson. Once I was president of NAC, I became a public figure. All the newspapers did profiles; from the Montreal *Gazette*'s "Rebel with Many Causes" to the *Globe and Mail*'s "NAC President a Radical Both Friends and Foes Say" to the *Toronto Star*'s "One Tough Fighter," the story was the same and pretty accurate, too. The *Star* tried to get me to pose wearing boxing gloves, but I declined. The media liked me because of my history with the pro-choice struggle and because they figured I'd make for good copy, so the profiles were very positive, which I have to admit made me feel pretty good.

In addition to announcing that NAC would be more radical and visible protesting in the streets, I was clear about my priorities as its new president. In Toronto, women of colour had been fighting for inclusion since the early 1980s and I had been part of that struggle in the IWD coalition. Through employment equity work, I understood the power of what today we would call "intersectional feminism," linking gender equality with equality for other oppressed groups. And my work with unions through the pro-choice movement helped me understand the power of working-class women. In my acceptance speech I said:

> The women's movement of the nineties is a different colour than the women's movement of the sixties. We are many colours, we are middle-class, working-class and poor women together, speaking French and

English and many other languages. We're young and old, able-bodied and disabled, lesbian and heterosexual, Native and non-Native. The women's movement has changed its face and now our challenge is to change our organizations to reflect this change.

My first act as president was to lead a march from the NAC annual general meeting in Ottawa, through the doors of Parliament, and up the stairs to the prime minister's office. There were no security barriers then. We barged up the stairs and made it to the waiting room "with a throng of placard-carrying women and demanded that Prime Minister Brian Mulroney answer to Canadian women," reported the Montreal *Gazette*.

The three major political parties had always met with the NAC lobby. It was a tradition. Women from across the country filled a room in one of the Parliament buildings and questioned the politicians. The party in power always attended, including key cabinet ministers. In the early days, the prime minister sometimes attended as well. Over the years, the lobby got more and more raucous, with women heckling and cheering the politicians' responses. It was an extraordinary exercise in democracy.

The year before I was acclaimed, the Mulroney government refused to attend the lobby for the first time. A group of us proposed that we march to Parliament Hill in protest, but the more moderate women argued that it was a mistake to cancel the lobby. After a heated debate, famed feminist Doris Anderson mediated a compromise. We would have the lobby but also march to Parliament Hill, right to the PM's door.

According to the *Gazette*, "NAC has been 'hijacked by extremists,' charged Senator Lowell Murray. The women's movement has returned to '60s-style tactics.'" It was an excellent start.

Soon after my acclamation, the Meech Lake Accord failed, largely because of Indigenous opposition. The first Indigenous member of a provincial legislature, Elijah Harper, refused to cast the vote for the unanimous consent required to amend the constitution. Instead, on June 22, 1990, he stood up in the Manitoba Legislative Assembly, holding an eagle feather. It was a powerful moment when Indigenous peoples rose up to stop a major government project.

Sandra Delaronde, a Métis woman who was newly elected to the NAC executive, had gotten me an invitation to speak at the rally outside the Manitoba Legislative Building. But what I remember is what Manitoba Regional Chief for the Assembly of First Nations Phil Fontaine said to the crowd: "We will pay a price for this, but it is a price we are willing to pay." It was an observation I remembered well when NAC took a leading role in opposing the next attempt to amend the constitution.

The fact that the first event I attended as NAC president was a First Nations rally was symbolic in some ways of my presidency. Indigenous women and women of colour had become more and more actively involved in the women's movement at the local level, especially in anti-violence groups but also on the International Women's Day Committee in Toronto. Yet NAC was still primarily a white women's organization. When I was elected president, three Indigenous women were also elected to the NAC executive:

Sandra Delaronde, Priscilla Settee from Saskatchewan, and Reanna Erasmus from the Northwest Territories. Indigenous women had been members of the NAC executive before, including pioneer activist Mary Two-Axe Earley, the first woman to fight the provisions of the Indian Act that discriminated against women. But three women meant a major presence.

At the first executive meeting, that presence was felt. One of the provincial representatives was a highly emotional and, in my view, dysfunctional person. At one point in the meeting, she burst out crying and ran out of the room. I just kept the discussion going but noticed that the Indigenous women looked uncomfortable.

"What's wrong?" I asked. "You seem uncomfortable."

After a moment of hesitation, Priscilla, the eldest of the group, responded, "Well, that's not how we do things."

"What do you do?"

"It's okay, this is your organization. We'll adapt."

"We want it to be your organization, too. What would you do?"

"Well, we think emotions are part of the meeting. If someone is upset, we want to know why."

Oh, brother. If a white woman had said that I would have put it down to New Age claptrap, but I really wanted the Indigenous women to feel they could contribute and that they were being heard. So I asked Priscilla if she would chair the meeting the next day and run it the way she thought it should be run.

Priscilla didn't want to chair the whole meeting, but she did offer to open the meeting with the suggestion that everyone say how they were feeling. Even though the women's movement promoted the notion that the personal is political, NAC was a fairly hierarchical and structured group. For me, keeping the personal and the political separate was a matter of survival, or so I thought.

The next day, Priscilla led the process and it was amazing. Instead of getting angry because of a fight with someone the night before or bursting into tears, women spoke openly about their concerns. If they were feeling happy, sad, angry, or disappointed, they told the group, and everyone was empathetic and supportive. I don't think I've ever seen a single action that so changed the tone of a meeting. What was famously a very fractious organization turned almost overnight into a much more cooperative one.

I quickly learned that if I wanted Indigenous women or women of colour to provide more leadership on the executive, I had to change my own leadership style. I had learned to lead from men. In many ways I had constructed myself to be a man in the way I worked, always sure of myself, never doubting. But now I was committed to sharing leadership with Indigenous women and women of colour, so I had to make space. That meant listening more and not always saying what I thought.

Oddly enough, my experience with the alters helped me to learn to listen. As I was learning to listen to the voices of my fragmented personality in my head, I learned to listen to the voices of other women on the executive. Three years later, when I stepped down as president, Carolann Wright-Parks, a Black anti-poverty activist who was often critical of me, paid tribute by saying, "What I love about Judy is her big ears." Everyone laughed, thinking that a big mouth was more like it, but she was telling me that I had indeed learned to listen. It helped open up NAC to more diverse voices. It also helped me become a more whole person.

BEING PRESIDENT OF NAC also meant that I had lots more time with Alvin and Glenna who two years before had moved from Guelph to Ottawa. Alvin had been my primary support for many years. This was not always an easy role, given both my ideological rigidity and my increasingly fragile mental health, but disclosure to him of my father's sexual abuse added a lot more tension. We all knew our father was difficult and sometimes violent. Alvin was more distant from him than either Leonard or I, but my disclosure of sexual abuse changed everything. My memories revealed such an enormous lie that it made everything suspect. Alvin felt as if he had lost his memory of childhood, which was now tainted by my memories.

I knew that Alvin needed time to figure out how to handle the disclosure of my abuse, and how to maintain a relationship with my parents, especially my mother, while he was supporting me. He also had to deal with the impact of my situation on his teenage daughters. At the time, I was so intensely involved in my own experiences that I didn't fully understand what Alvin was going through. I knew it was tough for him, but in preparing this memoir I asked him what it was like when I first told him about the abuse.

"At first I didn't believe anything," Alvin said. "I thought you were having a breakdown. It was traumatic for me, too.

I'm a person who copes with things. I just wanted it to go away. I'd been giving you support for many years, but this was very extreme and I didn't know how to cope with it. I just had to accept it. In a family, when something like this happens you can't prove it. I either had to accept it or deny it. I didn't want to believe it, but I had to support you. I thought to myself, *If I don't believe it, I am going to ruin my relationship with Judy, which she can't afford.* What was I to do? Was I not going to believe you and have you be all alone in this? You needed me to believe it."

Leonard was still estranged from the family. I did talk to him about the abuse memories, but I didn't see or communicate with him on a regular basis. I didn't see his children either. I used to take Lucas, his older boy, to the movies when he was little, but I hadn't seen him in a long time.

Alvin and Glenna were renting a lovely house in the Glebe area of Ottawa. It was a two-storey, three-bedroom house with the kitchen in the back, a very nice dining room, and a living room on the right of the entrance. Best of all, it was within walking distance of the canal. They had opened a terrific restaurant on Somerset Street that was almost instantly the haunt of bureaucrats and politicians. Thanks to my contacts, the staff of national unions also frequented the place.

Sometime later that summer, I was in Ottawa again. I was walking through the back door of the house into the kitchen. Alvin was standing at the sink. I can't remember what had happened to put me in the state I was in, but as soon as I closed the door I started to scream. It had happened in therapy and once in my apartment when I was alone, but it had never happened in front of other people. It came from somewhere deep inside of me and it was uncontrollable: once it started making its way out of my belly there was no way to stop it. The anguish of my wounds had become unbearable; it was as if it just exploded out of my body. I was so deep inside that pain that I couldn't see anything, couldn't think anything—I could only feel. So many years of holding down those feelings and now my worst nightmare was being realized: they were overwhelming me.

"It was a release of pain like someone who's grieving. Like someone seriously hurt," Alvin told me later. "You were wailing. Blood-curdling screams like a horror movie and then you were crying. The word I would use is 'anguish,' like something someone would do on hearing that their child died. It was completely out of control. It was scary. We knew you were in trouble, but it was the first time that it hit home how serious it was and how dangerous it was for you."

At the time, Alvin said to me, "Think of what's at stake. You're doing so well as president of NAC. You don't want to give that up, do you?" He was trying to talk me down. "Do you want me to call an ambulance?"

"No, not an ambulance," I whimpered. "It's stopping now." And then I just cried and cried. Afterwards I was exhausted.

This visit was also the first time the alters showed themselves to my family. I had explained that I was a multiple personality, but it didn't have much meaning until they saw it for themselves.

We were walking along the canal when I started talking in a child's voice. "Let's play horsey."

"Okay," a friend of the family replied, and I took off like a child riding a horse. She came right along with me. Alvin couldn't believe it, but it was harmless so he just put it out of his mind. There was only so much he could deal with.

Many years later when Svend Robinson, an NDP Member of Parliament, had a public breakdown that destroyed his political career, I realized that there but for the grace of I'm-not-sure-what I could have gone. I wouldn't have stolen a ring as he did; more likely, one of the alters would have started screaming, or during a press conference Sophie or Trouble could have shouted out at some journalist who was attacking me: "Stop being mean to Judy, you doodie head!"

But it never happened. I think there were two reasons. Marcia made an agreement with each alter: they would only come out in the office with her or with trusted friends. They existed to protect me. When she explained that I would get into trouble if they made themselves known publicly, they agreed to keep quiet. My ability to dissociate from my feelings served me well when I was in public. Even once I integrated the alters, I was able to dissociate from my feelings so I could calmly deal with a crisis. I had spent my life fighting every limitation that my upbringing, health, and status as a woman had imposed upon me. As Henry Morgentaler used to say when things got tough, "*Ne lâche pas.*" Never give up. And I never did.

The only significant impact on my work was that I couldn't stay at members' homes when I was travelling. Most of the members of the NAC executive had male partners. It was on a trip to New Brunswick that I realized that strange men could make the alters nervous. I spent two days struggling with them and urging them not to show themselves. After that, I had a talk with Alice, the executive director, and we agreed that from now on I would stay in hotels. My home away from home at Alvin and Glenna's place in Ottawa saved us a lot of money that we could spend on hotels in other cities. We explained to the other members that I needed my rest because I was travelling so much.

That summer, I was learning more about how the alters worked to protect me from my memories. One day, Sue and Gord were driving me up to their cottage when I yelled from the back seat: "Stop driving so fast, Gord. We'll get in an accident! Don't drive so fast!"

Gord answered me as if I were a child: "Don't worry, Judy. It's okay. I'm driving carefully, you don't have to worry." I immediately realized that it was one of the personalities that was scared. Later, I remembered being in a car accident when I was eleven years old. It had happened on the same highway at the same time of year. My father was driving and my *zeide* was sitting next to him in the front seat. Lenny and I were in the back. We were going to my grandparents' cottage near Lake Simcoe. It was raining and my father was probably driving too fast. The car started weaving. I was afraid to say anything even though I was scared. Suddenly I was on the ground. Both Lenny and I had been thrown out of the car through the passenger-side door, which had flown open. I had locked my door but Lenny hadn't locked his, and neither of us was wearing a seat belt. My father ran toward me, and then Lenny was standing behind him. Jack looked frightened and he was never scared. He picked me up from the ground where I had been thrown.

"Are you okay, Judy?" he asked, touching me to see if there were any broken bones or severe injuries. I couldn't talk for several hours.

I wasn't thinking about that accident while Gord was driving, but the alters were. This time, one of them decided to cry out to make sure there wouldn't be another accident.

THE PRICE THAT Phil Fontaine had alluded to at the Winnipeg rally came very quickly. On July 11, 1990, the Quebec police attacked a peaceful blockade by the Mohawk of Kanesatake. The Mohawk objected to the plans of the town of Oka to build a golf course on their traditional lands. The Mohawk warriors had arms but they had been advised by the Elders not to use them unless they were attacked. When the police threw tear gas and flash grenades at them, a firefight broke out. It is still unclear whether the police or the Mohawk fired first—I assume that means the police shot first. Police Corporal Marcel Lemay was shot and killed. The crisis escalated when the Quebec police set up barricades while the Mohawks received increasing support from Indigenous people across North America.

On July 30, I was invited to a rally at Oka at a peace camp set up just outside the barricades to welcome people. Hundreds of people, mostly Indigenous, came from across North America. After the rally, NAC worked hard to build support for the Mohawk. We took out a full-page ad in the *Globe and Mail*, co-sponsored by Greenpeace and the Canadian Peace Alliance, signed by hundreds of prominent Canadians, and organized a peace protest in Toronto in August.

Around this time, the alters stopped coming out, even in therapy. After so little time, it was unlikely that I had already integrated them. Then one day someone emerged.

"Who is it?" asked Marcia.

It was Trouble.

"Where have you all been?" It had been weeks since any of them had spoken to her or to me.

"We like it when Judy helps the Indians," he said.

"Why?"

"'Cause they was hurt like us."

Seventeen

TEETERING ON THE EDGE

IN DECEMBER 1990, work slowed down and I began to feel uneasy. Just before Christmas I wrote in my journal, "Today I went to the emergency ward of the hospital with chest pain, but really I think it is the pain in my heart from losing my family. I hope this Christmas I will get at least some of them back."

Alvin supported me, but there was a distance between us that hadn't been there before. On December 23, I drove to Ottawa through sleet and rain, worrying all the way there about whether the holidays would be strained. We had been celebrating Christmas ever since the girls were in daycare. Kael and Terra wanted to be like the other kids, and since neither Alvin nor Glenna was religious, they didn't see any reason why not. We decided that wherever we were, we would get together over the holidays, usually for at least five days. We always had a great time.

217

My job was to bring a new game for the family to play. Of course Alvin and Glenna, both professional cooks, did all the cooking. I worried my condition and the dramatic scenes of my last major visit would cause tension. I was relieved that it didn't. Things seemed more or less back to normal, and the alters stayed quiet. But still, something was bothering me.

At my request, Alvin and I went out for lunch. I asked him for advice about getting in touch with our mother. I still couldn't contact Jack, but I could talk to my mother and tell her what was going on. My idea was to ask her to come to Toronto. It had been a year since I cut off contact with my parents. Alvin agreed and said he would support me.

While I was in Ottawa with the family, I was calm, but once I returned home, the terrible dreams returned and the alters started emerging again.

In a session with Marcia, a new alter, Phoebe, came out and said she didn't like Alvin.

"He's a know-it-all," she told Marcia.

Phoebe was the most active one now and she had a lot of opinions. She didn't think therapy was doing me any good, but it had helped her a lot. Given that she was part of me, I didn't understand how she could decide that therapy was good for her but not for me. Maybe it made her feel important.

Lila, who had a Southern accent and was the only alter who clearly was not Jewish, said that she thought the problem was the evil inside me.

Then while I was driving home from therapy one day, a new personality emerged in a fury. When I got home, I raged a bit and felt weird all night, as if my veins and arteries had air in them. I felt very cold.

It turned out that it was the only adult personality. Marcia said the first time Julie Samuels emerged in therapy, she felt like someone had poured ice water over her head. Unlike the names of the other alters, I recognized the name Julie Samuels. It was a pseudonym I used in the RMG.

I believe that Julie Samuels emerged after the split in RWL. Before the depression, the stress of the polarized politics, the increasing distance from Ken, and perhaps the split in the organization produced a new personality. The young alters couldn't handle the complexity of the situation. While I had often dissociated in highly stressful situations, sometimes even losing time, I believe this was the only period after childhood during which a new personality emerged. And this personality was tough, cold, and distant, according to descriptions of friends at the time. No doubt I switched between that personality and what was left of me until I couldn't take it anymore. Less than a year later, I fell into a clinical depression.

The emergence of Julie Samuels shook me up. I started to wonder if there were more personalities, and if much of my life had been lived in different personas. There were several days of terrifying dreams. It seems these dreams were a significant part of the integration process. Even though I wrote down the dreams I could remember, I was thankful when I woke up and couldn't remember them. It was as if the pain had to find ways to escape, through the alters, through my dreams, through physical pain.

On January 4, I woke up with a start, scared and shivering,

at 4 a.m. I felt as if I was losing my definition and dissolving into many pieces. I was no longer sure of who I was, and who I would be at the end of this process.

"Who will I be when I come back together again?" I wrote in my journal. "Who will I be when the others are gone or integrated? Who will I be? Will my friends still like me? Will I still be able to be Judy Rebick? Who will I be? I am so afraid of losing the good with the bad and winding up just dead inside with no life at all."

THE WINTER OF 1991 was a very intense time in the world as well as in my private life. The greatest moment was the defeat of Mulroney's attempt to recriminalize abortion. On November 3, 1989, justice minister Kim Campbell had introduced Bill C-43, An Act Respecting Abortion. If Bill C-43 was approved by both the House of Commons and the Senate, it would become a criminal offence to induce an abortion on a woman unless it was done by, or under the direction of, a physician who considered that the woman's life or health was otherwise likely to be threatened. This time the doctor would be charged, not the patient, but it was a very restrictive law.

The day of the vote in the House of Commons, a group of young women stacked the gallery just as they had two decades before in the Abortion Caravan. In 1970, women had chained themselves to their seats, but this time security checks prevented them from bringing chains with them. Instead, as the vote was called, they started to scream at the old men for denying their reproductive rights. It had an enormous emotional impact on everyone who was there. Sitting in the gallery next to them, I could feel their pain deep in my belly. Security asked them to leave, but they refused and had to be dragged out. Regardless, it didn't change the vote.

We thought we still had a chance to pressure the Senate so NAC worked with the pro-choice movement to organize a National Day of Action for Choice on October 13, 1990. We also made a presentation to the Senate committee. Usually when we presented to a parliamentary committee, the Conservatives attacked us, the NDP supported us, and the Liberals sometimes supported us and sometimes didn't. This time was different. I felt all the senators were seriously questioning us about the impact of the proposed law.

On a cold February day, Norma Scarborough and I watched the Senate vote. I was holding my breath. They called out the names of the senators, who would respond yea or nay. According to the rules, a tie would defeat the motion. The pro-choice senators in all the parties had worked hard to sway their colleagues, but there were still quite a few anti-choice senators. Furthermore, Mulroney had made it clear to his caucus that he wanted this bill passed. We listened to each yea and nay, but it was so close we didn't know the outcome until the Speaker announced in a booming voice, "The resolution fails!"

We cheered. This was the first time since the 1940s that the unelected Senate had defeated a bill. The final credit went to Senator Pat Carney, who flew in from Vancouver to vote against the bill. As a very senior Conservative cabinet minister, she had shepherded the Free Trade Agreement of the Americas—hardly an ally in the past. Now she was a senator, but she was still in the Cabinet. She knew the price she would pay for her vote, but she was pro-choice. Once again we had evidence of the importance of the pro-choice issue to most women.

I was also deeply involved in speaking out against the Mulroney government on a number of other issues. The 1991 Gulf War was a major concern. Women's peace groups were an important part of NAC. The Voice of Women, a pioneer women's group founded in 1960, had always focused on anti-war activity. They used to drive me crazy, calling me every time I used words like "struggle" or "fight" in my media appearances. Even "strategy," it seems, was a militarist word. But I agreed with them that NAC should mobilize against the Gulf War, and we pulled off a cross-country anti-war action with a focus on mobilizing women and children.

It was through these efforts that I got to know Michael Manolson, the executive director of Greenpeace. NAC, Greenpeace, and the Canadian Peace Alliance organized big anti-war demonstrations across the country. Michael called me from the airport the day we learned that the bombing had started in mid-January 1991. Both of us were upset so I invited him over to watch the news together.

At the end of the evening, he kissed me good night. I asked him to stay. He told me that he was afraid he'd disappoint me, that he needed time to process what had happened. That was probably better for me, too. The Judy who could easily have sex with anyone she felt attracted to was gone. Now there were the others, the alters, to consider. I was up all night. The intimate moment had produced incredibly intense feelings in me. I hadn't felt like this in years. It all seemed too good to be true. He was gentle, kind, sensitive, and an equal in every way. We seemed to really connect.

I asked the alters whether there was anyone who was worried.

NO FINE WITH US, FUN. MICHAEL IS NOT SCARY AT ALL.

It's true; Michael wasn't scary but he was a bit of a womanizer. We had a deep connection, no doubt, but he was unreliable and that triggered a lot of insecurities in me. After a couple of intense connections and withdrawals, Trouble came out and said, "There is no way I am going to let you be with Michael. We're only safe when we are alone."

Michael wanted the emotional connection, but he wasn't sure he wanted a relationship. I started to shut down, which worried me. I wanted to feel my feelings now, not shut them down in fear. The dance of intimacy and withdrawal continued until we decided it was better to remain friends.

I was travelling almost constantly in 1991. In March alone, I was in Ottawa a couple of times; St. John's, Newfoundland; Halifax; and Vancouver. After a while my anger started to resurface—inappropriate anger, especially at the NAC staff who were complaining that we were doing too much. At one point, Alice de Wolff said she was designing a harness that would hold me back. She argued that if I kept getting the organization involved in issues when there weren't enough resources, we would wind up with a reputation of being ineffective.

In mid-March the following entry appeared in my journal:

Things that Sophie and Trouble like to do:
Dance
Laugh
Run
Hug (not Trouble but only for Judy)
Funny movies
Children
Hot bath
Rob
Kael
Yell

I wasn't doing any of those things except the baths and the yelling, but I don't think it was the kind of yelling they meant.

At the beginning of April, I started to feel out of control. The first sign of it was yelling at Michael for being three hours late for what was supposed to be a day trip. The next day I got angry at almost everyone, from the dry cleaner who didn't have my clothes ready to the NAC staff. On April 10, I wrote, "Freaking out, feeling so abandoned and alone. Need someone to help me. No one cares about me."

Exactly one month later, on May 10, I wrote, "One month since the freak-out. Now I feel like I am a flower opening up to the sun filled with joy and excitement then comes the fear in the night. Then comes the putrid fear that closes up my budding joy."

AS THE YEAR progressed, alters seemed to come and go. Phoebe, who had been so prominent, receded, and in her place was Sophie, who was more fun-loving and less angry. Later that summer, Sophie asked Marcia if she could meet Rob. Of all my friends, the alters liked Rob best. Rob was a lot younger than I was. I had met him at the Coalition for Employment Equity and we became friends after we both went to Ottawa by train in 1988 to participate in an action against free trade.

A couple of alters had already talked to him on walks without asking. Because he had worked with abused children, he understood what I was going through better than anyone else, including me. He hadn't dealt with multiple personality disorder before, and wasn't quite sure what to make of it, but he knew that as a friend he had to support me to get through this terrible process. If holding hands with a woman twenty years his senior talking excitedly on the way to the ice cream store was required, that was what he would do. But Sophie wasn't satisfied with the odd conversation. She wanted to have a real talk with him, one that was arranged by me. Marcia said it would be okay.

Rob and I went out for a drink on Queen Street West, a hip part of Toronto. I explained to him that Sophie wanted to meet him. As soon as I said the words, I started to feel very nervous. I was always relaxed with Rob and nervous was not a very common state for me, so I suspected Sophie was anxious to get going. He agreed. I thought the meeting should take place in my apartment in private. As we were driving along Queen West, I asked Rob, "What are those people doing?" I was already Sophie. It was after work and people were jogging along the street. Sophie hadn't been out in the world for a long time, so many things were unfamiliar to her.

Rob parked on the street just behind my apartment. At six feet two inches, he usually had to slow down so I could keep up with him, but this time I was way ahead of him, almost running.

"I realized it wasn't you when you bounded up the stairs two at a time," he told me later. "You would never do that."

Rob sat down at one end of the couch and Sophie at the other end, suddenly shy. I only remember one part of the conversation.

"Why won't you be Judy's boyfriend?" Sophie asked him earnestly.

"I like Judy very much," he responded with a smile, "but I already have a girlfriend." She seemed satisfied with that answer.

I have a memory of coming back into the room and seeing Sophie on the couch with Rob. It was a strange out-of-body experience.

"What was it like?" I asked him, now back to myself.

"It was like you introduced me to a friend and then left the room."

"How could that be? It's my body."

"I don't know but that's how it felt."

I didn't know either.

My friendship with Rob was part of a habit I had started many years before: intimate friendships with men without sex. After my relationship with Ken, I never had another boyfriend. I had a few lovers, but most of my relationships

226

with men were close friendships without benefits. I don't know very many other women my age who have such close friendships with men who aren't ex-lovers or the partners of female friends. The closest relationships in my childhood were with my brothers, which was how I explained the friendships to myself, but looking back on my life I realize that from the time I began to uncover the memories I was unable to combine sex and emotional intimacy. When it came to romance, I started late and finished early.

Eighteen

THE BEST OF TIMES

IN THE LAST FEW years, NAC had faced multiple crises but the most important one to me was the division with the Fédération des Femmes du Québec (FFQ) over the Meech Lake Accord. The year before my presidency, I, along with Barbara Cameron, a left-wing political science professor from York University in Toronto, had fought for NAC to support the distinct society clause in the accord. Barbara and I both believe that Quebec is a nation within Canada that has the right to self-determination. However, many of the women who had fought for gender rights in the constitution during the 1980s believed that the distinct society clause undermined women's rights.

The debate within the organization was brutal. Finally, NAC reached a compromise supporting the distinct society clause but opposing the Meech Lake Accord because it threatened new social programs by decentralizing federal power to all the provinces. In Quebec, the details were unimportant. According to the Quebec media, the women's movement in Canada helped to bring down the Meech Lake Accord, which all of Quebec, including the Quebec women's movement, supported. The FFQ quit NAC. They claimed it wasn't because of Meech Lake, but I believed that it was. So it was a priority for me to solve the problem and find a way to rebuild unity with Quebec women.

Knowing that Mulroney would be making another attempt to amend the constitution to include Quebec, we set up a committee to develop a new position on the constitution. What was coming was dubbed the "Canada Round." Meech Lake was focused almost entirely on Quebec; this round would address Indigenous rights, Senate reform, and Quebec's status as a distinct society within Canada. All the groups who felt left out—Indigenous people, triple-E (equal, elected, effective) Senate advocates from Alberta, women—would feel included.

The NAC committee was made up of an extraordinary group of women, including Monique Simard, vice-president of the Confédération des syndicats nationaux (CSN), the large public sector union in Quebec; Madeleine Parent, a legendary Quebec trade unionist; Sandra Delaronde, the young Métis woman who was a member of the NAC executive and a genius mediator; Shelagh Day, a human rights activist; Saloumé Lucas, representing Women Working with Immigrant Women; and Barbara Cameron. Monique would go on to become president and general director of the Parti Québécois and a leader of the Yes side in the 1995 referendum on Quebec sovereignty. And a great friend of mine.

"I couldn't understand how she could think of setting up her own country when they hadn't dealt with the fact that it wasn't their land," Sandra told me later.

Barbara, who had been fighting for Quebec's right to self-determination for years, insisted that the rest of Canada would also have to understand itself as a nation, instead of assuming that Canada included Quebec and First Nations. She understood colonialism better than the rest of us Anglos in English Canada.

The committee came up with what was quite an advanced position: Canada was composed of three nations, each of which was multi-ethnic and multicultural and each of which had the right to self-determination. We realized that there were multiple nations among Indigenous people, but that wasn't argued as strongly in the early 1990s as it is today. Our position was that Canada should negotiate nation-to-nation, thus rejecting the country's existing colonial relationships. We managed to convince NAC's membership and much of the labour movement to support the position. It had many implications for the next constitutional debate, in which we were to play an important role.

ALL THIS INTENSE activism kept the alters mostly at bay. I still went to see Marcia every week, and in addition to being president of NAC, I was still working at CHS. I was always exhausted. More than once I wrote in my journal, "I am just too tired to live." I found out through later research that dissociation, which had now become a daily occurrence, usually when I was at home alone, takes a lot of physical energy. Constantly reliving episodes of abuse in therapy, even if it was through the alters, was also exhausting. I never planned anything after a therapy session; I always needed time to recover.

In the years before I became president of NAC, I was part of an unsuccessful fight to pay the president. Because it was in essence a full-time volunteer position, only privileged women could do it. I didn't have a husband or the ability to go on sabbatical leave so I had to continue working. Luckily Denis Morrice, my boss at CHS, gave me whatever time I needed to do my work at NAC, but it was getting ridiculous. Understandably, he was starting to put pressure on me to do more work for CHS. I told the executive committee that unless we could get the organization to agree to pay me, I couldn't do the job anymore. As we had started working on independent fundraising for the first time and people did not want me to leave, the executive agreed to pay the president, a decision approved at the 1991 AGM. I was paid half time in 1991 and then full time in 1992. That made all the difference.

At the annual general meeting we made two other big changes. We increased the president's term from one to two years. It meant that I was the first NAC president to serve for three years, one one-year term and one two-year term. The second issue we agreed on was getting more women of colour onto the executive committee. Having lobbied for employment equity at the federal and provincial levels, as well as developing an affirmative action program at CHS to get more deaf people into management positions, I was an expert in the field. But it was difficult to achieve affirmative action in a mostly voluntary organization.

After a lot of discussion, we decided to designate at least one member at large from the more populous provinces and one vice-president who was an immigrant woman, woman of colour, disabled woman, or Indigenous woman. If someone from one of these groups did not fill the position, the position was left empty. We also designated one vice-president from Quebec—that had always been a tradition but now we formalized it.

The transformation of the executive was dramatic. For the first time we had a representative of women with disabilities in the person of Joan Meister from British Columbia, a trade union activist, and former president of the DisAbled Women's Network (DAWN). We also had strong leadership from women of colour, including Carolann Wright-Parks, a Black activist originally from Halifax, now an anti-poverty activist in Toronto; Felé Villacin, a very sophisticated immigrant activist who worked with domestic workers; Winnie Ng, an indefatigable activist who had a long history of organizing immigrant women in the labour movement; Amy Go, who had worked with immigrant women and the Chinese Canadian National Council; and Flora Fernandez, who worked in a shelter in Montreal.

The following year, Sunera Thobani, a brilliant and articulate young woman from BC who would take over as president, joined the executive. The vice-president was Monique Simard from Quebec; Sandra Delaronde was the designated VP; and Yvonne Stanford, an anti-war activist from Alberta, and Shelagh Day were also VPs. Along with Trish Walsh from Newfoundland, who had led the occupation of the secretary of state's offices, and my old friend and comrade Jackie Larkin from BC, it was a feminist dream team. We would need that strength in the months to come.

IN AUGUST 1991, the Supreme Court of Canada struck down the rape shield law. Enacted in 1982 after fierce lobbying by women's groups, the rape shield law prevented the questioning of a rape victim about her sexual history. The Supreme Court ruled that this restriction violated the rights of the accused. Justice minister Kim Campbell announced that she would rapidly replace the law.

NAC member groups that worked on violence against women called together a number of women's groups to develop a proposal for the minister. We decided that the key problem in rape cases, which resulted in a very low rate of conviction, was the question of consent. Most accused rapists claimed they believed there was consent and then it was his word against hers. Since the sexual assault laws would have to be rewritten, we decided to push for the inclusion of consent in the law. NAC and the Legal Education Action Fund (LEAF) got a meeting with Campbell and invited key representatives from grassroots violence against women groups to attend. It was a diverse and powerful group, a sign of how sophisticated the women's movement had become. Campbell was so eager for our support, she called me herself to talk about the meeting in advance.

This was the first time I had worked with Lee Lakeman. Lee was legendary in the women's movement. She had established one of the first women's shelters in Ontario in 1972, by moving into the basement of her own home and turning the main floor into a shelter. After moving to Vancouver, she joined Vancouver Rape Relief, which maintains a militant approach to ending violence against women to this day, although not without controversy, most recently for its trans-exclusionary politics. She was tough and did not suffer fools easily. Most of what I had heard about her was negative. She fought fiercely for what she believed in and she didn't think much of NAC, which she saw as an organization of mostly middle-class, privileged women who didn't focus enough on issues of violence. Once I realized that a large proportion of NAC member groups were anti-violence groups, I agreed with her. And now that I was finally dealing with my father's abuse, I was more able to address the issues associated with violence against women and children than I had in the past.

Our meeting started with the bureaucrats. They informed us that Campbell was anxious to pass a law before Parliament rose for the Christmas holidays. They agreed with our position on consent, but it would be impossible to draft an acceptable law which included a definition of consent before the holidays. We argued that without a definition of consent, they would not have our support.

Lee asked them to leave so we could consult among ourselves before meeting with the minister. I was shocked by her chutzpah. These were senior bureaucrats, including the deputy minister, and she basically ordered them out of the room.

I knew how to stand up to the government, even to a minister or prime minister, but negotiations were not my strong point. Lee was a tough negotiator and I respected her expertise on the issue so I supported her. Not only did she insist that we keep our position on consent, but she felt we couldn't legitimately claim to represent the women's movement with so few women in the room.

When justice minister Kim Campbell arrived, we let the lawyers among us explain how we could include consent in the law. Lee and I made clear that a law that did not define consent would not be acceptable to us. Our experience told us that a definition of consent would result in more convictions in sexual assault cases. It was the only time in my life that I witnessed a minister change her mind in front of a lobby group.

"Okay, my lawyers will work with your lawyers and come up with a definition of consent that will pass muster," Campbell said.

I was elated. But Lee was not yet satisfied. She would not let the minister leave without agreeing to pay for a national meeting of anti-violence groups every year. Campbell agreed. Lee understood this was a rare moment where we had a lot of power. The minister wanted this bill to be her legacy, especially after what she saw as the disaster of the failed abortion law, where she introduced a new abortion bill that was defeated in the Senate. She wanted to be seen as a champion of women and needed our support to get the bill through Parliament. Lee sensed that and pushed. It blew my mind.

We had scheduled a press conference right after the meeting so we got to announce the agreement and put further pressure Campbell to make good on her word.

At the press conference, a LEAF lawyer explained the proposal for the new law. A *Toronto Star* reporter asked her, "So is this a No Means No law?"

Seeing a front-page headline I stepped in. "We're talking about a law which says no means no and yes means yes and before you initiate sexual contact it's your responsibility to find out if it's yes or no."

"Proposed rape law's message: No means no," read the *Toronto Star* headline, and the article's lead sentence was "Canada could soon have a new rape law with a stern warning for men: No means no." It was front-page news, not only because it was a bold move on the part of a woman justice minister, but also because NAC had never agreed with the Mulroney government on anything before. It was a remarkable coup for us, made possible only by a collective effort led by the anti-violence activists.

In the spring of 1992, the new rape law was passed in the House of Commons with rare unanimous consent. While it was an important victory at the time, we've found out since that the problem is much more deeply rooted and defining consent was not enough to secure more rape convictions.

DURING THIS TIME, Marcia and I began the process of integration. I had to accept that each of these personalities was part of me, and instead of resisting their anger, fear, and desire for more fun, I had to learn to allow for those feelings and desires. As a result of this work, more and more memories were beginning to emerge.

A key memory was something that took place after we moved to the three-bedroom apartment on East 94th

Street in Brooklyn. I got the room off the kitchen. I remember always being scared in that room. In the sessions with Marcia, the alters showed me why.

This room was on the opposite side of the house from my parents' bedroom. My father had much more freedom there than in the tiny basement apartment at my grandmother's house. I remember he would tell me to lie on my stomach and rub himself against my back. I felt as if I was suffocating. Then one day he turned me over and forced open my legs. In therapy I heard only the voices of the alters, not his responses.

"What are you doing, Daddy?" said Mary in her sweetest voice.

"I don't like this, Daddy. Can't I lie on my tummy?" pleaded Lila.

Then Lobo appeared, trying to slip out from under him to run away.

"I'm afraid, Daddy." It was Sophie. "I really, really don't like this. This is really bad. I think you should stop. Mommy will be mad at you."

Then HIM: "Stop it, you bastard! Stop it right now!"

"I'm sick, Daddy. Really sick." Trouble this time. "I'm gonna puke. I'm gonna puke."

Then Porsha started to scream and scream and scream.

It was like listening to a play. One after another the personalities would appear and then disappear with another one taking his or her place. Marcia had explained that I had created the alters to defend myself against the abuse, but this was the first time that I actually saw how they did it. Each tactic of resistance was represented by another personality.

When one didn't work, another took up the battle. Finally, Porsha was successful.

"I didn't stop screaming," Porsha said proudly. "He tried to put his hand over my mouth but I bit him. That served him right."

He stopped. He stood up beside the bed just before my mother came to the door.

"I don't know what's wrong with her," my father told her. "I was having my coffee and she just started screaming and wouldn't stop."

"I hate it here, Mommy. I don't want to stay here anymore. I hate it! I hate it!" Porsha told her. That's when my mother agreed to move me in with Lenny. Little Alvin would stay in the room off the kitchen.

To this day I don't know if that was the last time my father abused me. No other scenes of abuse emerged in therapy, and once we moved to Toronto I have almost no memories of my father inside the house. I imagine that this was too close a call and he decided to stop.

The main thing I remember about the house on East 94th Street was the nightmares. I often woke up screaming, convinced that monsters were coming out of the wall. I can still see the shadows in the room I shared with Lenny. My father came in to comfort and quiet me by turning on the light. "See," he would say, "no monsters." But somehow I wasn't comforted.

My mother never came.

Nineteen

THE FINAL CONFRONTATION

WHILE PRIVATELY I WAS in the process of reintegrating my fragmented self, publicly I was working with NAC to prepare for a series of constitutional negotiations, for what later would be known as the Charlottetown Accord. Blaming the defeat of the Meech Lake Accord as a failure to communicate with Canadians, Mulroney's government decided to set up a series of constitutional conferences to debate each of their primary proposals in the Canada Round. NAC was among the seventy-five community organizations invited. In addition, there were about fifty places for "ordinary Canadians" who applied by mail and were chosen by lottery. The other 220 participants were experts and politicians.

On January 17, 1992, on the way to the conference in Halifax, which was to deal with the division of powers among the provinces, I ran into Judge Rosie Abella on the plane. Abella was not yet a Supreme Court justice, but she had a high profile because of her work as Commissioner of the Royal Commission on Equality in Employment in the 1980s. I'm not sure how I had made her acquaintance, but I knew her well enough to call her Rosie. She was the chair of the conference so I decided to approach her. She was sitting in business class and I asked her if she would be open to chatting with me.

Soon after the plane took off, Rosie slipped back into economy and took the empty seat next to mine. We chatted for a while and then I explained our position.

"We're worried about the devolution of power to the provinces that some of the premiers are proposing," I said. "We'll never get a national child care program if it is up to each province. We need a strong federal government. At the same time, we realize that Quebec wants more power, and as a nation within Canada they should have it. Our position is to give Quebec the powers they want but to keep a strong federal state. Different powers for Quebec."

"Is it fair constitutionally for Quebec to have more power than the other provinces?" she asked. "You know a lot of people have opposed this as special powers for one province."

"We think it's fair. None of the other provinces claims to be a nation as Quebec does. Our framework is that Canada is a nation of nations, each of which has the right to self-determination. By treating all the provinces equally we wind up with a devolution of power, which is certainly not what women want and I don't think most people in the other provinces want it either. I know you understand treating everyone the same does not produce equality."

"That position is being put forward by some academics

as well," she said. "What I can promise is that I'll make sure there is open space for a discussion."

She kept her promise.

I arrived in Halifax convinced that the government would stack the conference with people supporting its position. But we had supporters from the labour movement, other advocacy groups, and academics as well. Needless to say the Quebec delegates were pleasantly surprised that anyone outside the province would support their position.

The presence of ordinary Canadians changed the tone of the discussion. Instead of the usual Kabuki-style theatre of polemic debate, each group had to convince individual citizens who didn't hold a strong a position. Persuasion rather than gang warfare dominated the debate. It was refreshing.

During the introductory remarks in the workshop I was in, a middle-aged woman from New Brunswick said to me, "Get away from me. I'm sick of hearing about Quebec. They are always demanding things and making things worse for the rest of us."

But in the workshop Senator Gérald Beaudoin from Quebec explained that the province didn't really want to take anything away from the rest of Canada; it just wanted autonomy in certain areas. I explained that what we were proposing was that Quebec would get the powers it wanted but the rest of us would keep a strong central government. It was a win-win situation where everyone got what they wanted.

After listening to the discussion, the woman from New Brunswick changed her mind: "Well, I don't mind if Quebec gets what they want, as long we in New Brunswick get what we want."

When we brought the resolution to the floor, Thomas d'Aquino from the Business Council on National Issues, who became our primary opponent in all the conferences, tried to raise a point of order to defeat our motion. Rosie Abella ruled him out of order.

Much to our astonishment, our proposal won the conference by a significant majority. Thereafter, almost all the conferences resulted in the rejection of the federal government's positions and proposing solutions more to our liking. Most important was the decision at the Calgary conference to adopt proportional representation in the Senate and at the Toronto conference where the focus was on self-government for Indigenous peoples.

After the final conference in Vancouver in February, there was a new energy around the constitutional conferences, best expressed by *Toronto Star* columnist Michele Landsberg: "Wait a minute — how did constitutional conferences, once the national soporific, suddenly become a wellspring of new energy? A sea-change has happened, a lifting of the doom cloud. 'It's the women,' my husband kept exclaiming, as he watched the five conferences on TV. 'They're turning it around.'"

We were elated, but the legal responsibility for constitutional reform lay with the premiers and the federal government. They discussed the proposals that emerged from the conferences behind closed doors and came back with something altogether different. In the end, the Charlottetown Accord rejected our proposal for different powers for Quebec, instead supporting the devolution of power. It also supported an elected Senate but left it to the provinces to decide how to elect their senators, and recommended a form of self-government for Indigenous peoples. NAC opposed the Accord and successfully organized for the No side in a referendum on the matter.

DURING THE CHARLOTTETOWN ACCORD conferences, my brother Leonard visited my parents in Florida and told them that I had remembered my father's abuse. I was furious at him for breaking a confidence, but mostly I felt helpless and devastated. After almost twenty years, I started smoking again.

I knew now that I had to talk to my mother. In January 1992, in the middle of these intense conferences, I had a speaking engagement at a National Organization for Women conference in Miami. Fort Lauderdale, where my parents lived, wasn't far away. Alvin agreed to come to Florida at the same time to lend me support.

Marcia felt I was not yet ready to confront my father. The week before I left, I had a somewhat prophetic dream. I am sitting with the family around a big round table. Suddenly, an angry personality emerges and begins screaming at my father. He is taken aback but looks resigned. I am out of control and say to Leonard, "Get me out of here," and he does.

Alvin and my mother arrived at my hotel just after lunch. My mother looked a little uncomfortable but otherwise calm. We kissed on the cheek as usual.

"I'm sorry I haven't talked to you in so long, Mom, but I've been going through a terrible time."

She nodded, indicating that she understood.

"About two years ago, I started having memories," I said. "At first I didn't want to believe it, but it soon became clear that I was a little girl being abused. The person abusing me was Dad."

My voice was shaking. I felt a little ill. At first she said nothing. She was sitting at the end of the bed and I was on a chair facing her. Alvin was a little distance away.

"It started at Grandma's house and continued in that room on East 94th Street. That's why I was so scared to stay in that room." Fear slipped into my breast. This could be the end of my relationship with my mother.

As I spoke her face transformed. I could see the horror of what I was telling her about my father, her husband, was beginning to sink in.

She started speaking slowly. "It was a time that I was worried about him. He was acting kind of crazy during those years, getting angry for no reason. Lashing out all the time, getting into fights. I thought it was because he was unhappy at work. It's why I agreed to move to Toronto."

"I didn't remember until now so maybe he didn't remember what he did either." I explained dissociation to her and how given that his father physically and emotionally abused him, he might have dissociated from his traumatic experiences, too. I didn't disclose the multiple personalities to her. I figured it would be too much for her.

"Will you come and talk to your dad?" Even after what I told her, he was still her most important concern.

"No, I don't think that's a good idea." I explained how I was healing and didn't want to do anything that would set me back.

"Please." She was begging now. "We need our family back. You've got to talk to him, please."

I said I would think about it, and she and Alvin got up to leave. Alvin gave me a hug.

Later Alvin wrote down his experience of the meeting. His main observation was that it was as if my mother and I were having two totally different conversations; it was as if we were in different rooms talking about different subjects. He saw our tragic inability to communicate with each other.

She didn't apologize or say anything remotely compassionate to me. She didn't get angry with me or reject me. She believed me, at least in that moment. And she knew it was wrong. That was, in part, what I needed. Opening her arms and holding me, gently stroking my head and crying with me would have been good, but that wasn't my mother. How I longed for that mother.

After she left, I called Marcia to ask her opinion about seeing my father.

"I don't think you're ready, Judy. Really, it's very risky. Maybe next time."

After I hung up, I thought, *What next time? Alvin is here now. I don't think I could do it on my own.* My mother had never begged me to do anything for her. He must be making her life hell. And talking to her hadn't set me back. I hadn't heard from the alters or lost time or had an anxiety attack. I was fine.

IN THE MORNING, I drove my rental car to my parents' place. It was a thirty-minute drive but it felt like hours.

Staring out the windshield with my hands glued to the steering wheel, I drove the familiar route to their suburban condo. My chest felt as if it would explode. I was terrified. Never in my life have I felt more afraid to come face to face with Jack, the villain of my alters' imaginations. But I didn't turn back.

My parents lived in a comfortable two-bedroom town-house in one of the residential complexes springing up all over the suburbs of Fort Lauderdale. Alvin greeted me at the door. We walked by the kitchen and the dining room on the right; the bedroom where I usually stayed was on the left. There in the living room in his La-Z-Boy chair was Jack. It was my father's energy that made him so attractive to people, but now that energy was gone. His graceful body had shrunken to an almost skeletal form. He seemed feeble. Of course I knew he was old, but I think the alters had to see that he could no longer hurt me. My fear lifted.

Alvin took me to the four-seater couch next to Jack. It was a strange place for such a confrontation. Like most of these apartments in Florida, everything was soft pastel and soft pillows. My mother was sitting on a chair opposite. I was closest to my father but on the far side of the couch.

Alvin held my hand and I began.

"I think you know why I'm here."

Jack said nothing, which was something new. I had no idea what he was thinking or feeling. I held Alvin's hand tighter. Alvin was keeping me in the room, preventing me from dissociating. It was all I could do to stay present.

My first emotion was anger. "I've been going through a lot. Two years ago I started remembering what you did to

248

me. I was only five years old when you got me to touch you. Only five years old. How could you?"

He found his strength to challenge me. "What do you mean by 'touch'? What kind of touch?"

I stood my ground. "You made me touch your penis."

"I didn't do that. That's disgusting. I would never do such a thing."

"And that was just the beginning. It got much worse when we moved to East 94th Street."

"Stop." He collapsed into his chair. "I didn't do that. I don't know why you're saying that." Now he was quieter. My mother might have been giving him signs to shut up.

I was having trouble speaking. My heart was pounding so hard that I could barely hear anything else. I didn't want to start crying in front of them; I didn't want to show him my pain. But the confrontation was overwhelming, and I started to regress. I was becoming a small child. I couldn't think of what to say. I was confused.

Finally, I managed to say one more thing before I became a child, confused, scared, and sad: "I'm sorry I didn't remember earlier, because then you would have suffered all your life instead of me suffering."

My mother spoke for the first time: "Okay then, can we put all this behind us now?"

Even now as I write this, my heart is broken.

"Judy and I are leaving now," Alvin said. He took my hand and led me out. Once we were outside, he put his arms around me and I wept. He held me as the grief overwhelmed me.

"Do you want me to drive you back to the hotel?"

"No, I'm okay," I said.

When I got home I wrote in my journal: "Is this the final chapter? He never questioned that I had been abused. It was a pathetic defence. Confronted him and got over the fear. Got back my mom.

"Brave new world. I am not alone and Alvin was wonderful, just wonderful."

Despite having confronted my father, not much changed. The alters did not see the old man sitting in his easy chair as the Jack who terrified them. Perhaps they realized he was gone for good.

A FEW MONTHS later, the "false memory syndrome" controversy made the news, causing a backlash against recovered childhood memories. The so-called syndrome has never been proven and has since been discredited, but both my parents grabbed on to it as a way of maintaining that the abuse never happened without blaming me. The therapist must have influenced me, they said. I had had flashes of the memories before I went to Marcia, but they didn't want to hear that. Denial was always my mother's modus operandi.

I talked to my mother now and then on the telephone, but I never went to Florida again. Alvin and Glenna had moved back to Guelph after their Ottawa restaurant went bankrupt. A couple of years later, my parents moved to Guelph, so that Alvin could help my mother deal with my father's illnesses. Alvin said it was up to me whether I wanted to see them and he would support whatever decision I made. After much deliberation, I decided that not seeing them now that I was feeling better would be abusive on my part, but I remained wary around my father and kept my distance. My relationship with my mother remained strained until her ninety-fifth year, the year that she died.

My father died for me that day in Florida. The day he actually died, some ten years later, I felt nothing. I was in Costa Rica on holiday and couldn't get back for the funeral. It's the only good thing my father ever did for me, I would joke. Even my fiercest feminist friends couldn't understand how I could feel nothing when my father died. "Why should I feel anything for a man who violated and betrayed me?" I said. Now I realize that I experienced the grief of losing my father that day in Florida. Jack, the bogeyman of my childhood alters, was so tied up with my charismatic, funny, brave, exciting father that once the fear was gone so was the love. And he didn't fight for his daughter. He just let me go.

Epilogue

IS IT OVER?

FOLLOWING MY TRIP to Florida, I made a lot of progress in therapy. After confronting my father, I was able to bring the different fragments of my personality together. One by one, each alter disappeared. That summer, I had another prophetic dream.

I am in the backyard with my old lover Jeremiah. High up in a tree is a little boy. Jeremiah says to the little boy, "Revenge. You want revenge. Come on down here." The boy laughs and climbs down. He is very small but sturdy with a fierce look on his face and dark skin. He is only big enough to be three or four, but he has the manner of an older child. He looks at me fiercely and then over the fence where there are other children. He looks again, turns, walks away, and climbs over the fence. All the children are cheering.

Later in therapy, I found out the boy was Trouble, the one who was most afraid of my relationships with men. He had taken his leave. By that time, only Sophie remained. And at some point, she, too, was gone. As Marcia had predicted, I had integrated the alters. I was now the guardian Simon, the playful Lobo, the skeptical Phoebe, the fun-loving Sophie, the furious HIM, and the five others, too. Whenever I feel sick or fatigued, I stop to rest and see what's wrong. Sometimes the source is physical and sometimes it's emotional, but it's no longer Trouble.

My superpowers have mostly deserted me, too. I get scared now—my fearlessness is gone. But I can still dissociate in a dangerous situation. In January 2009, I was one of eight Jewish women who occupied the Consulate General of Israel in Toronto to protest Israel's attack on Gaza. I was in charge of negotiating with the police. We got in by pretending to be tourists. Once all eight of us were inside, we sat on the floor and declared, "We are occupying the consulate in protest of Israel's attack on Gaza."

Instantly, a wall came down around us protecting the staff from the threat. Two security guards ordered us to leave.

"We're not leaving," I said.

One of the younger women declared, "We're not leaving until Israel leaves Gaza."

The older security guard grabbed one of her legs and started dragging her out.

"Take your hands off her!" I ordered him in my warrior voice. In the meantime another woman was filming the whole scene with her smartphone. When the guard saw her, he ran over, slapped her across the face, and grabbed her phone. That's when the dissociation kicked in.

"Do you know who we are? You're looking at some very prominent women in Canada. If you touch one of us again, you're going to jail," I said calmly, but firmly.

"Forget it," he sneered. "You're on Israeli territory now. Canadian law can't protect you."

"This is a consulate, not an embassy. It is not Israeli territory," I proclaimed with total certainty, having no idea whether what I said was true or not. It's not, but it's amazing how people will believe you if you speak with confidence.

"Well then," he stuttered, "we pay the rent here and we want you out."

"We're not going anywhere until the police force us to."

"They've already been called."

"Fine."

Then the other security guard, silent until then, said, "I'm a police officer."

"Let's see your ID," I demanded. When he showed his RCMP credentials, I said, "Get him out of here." And he did.

Once the police arrived they were very polite, supportive even. Nevertheless they handcuffed us and put us in the police wagon for almost an hour. In the meantime, our supporters had gathered at the back of the building, where the police had escorted us out.

We had a support network that was getting updates and sending out media releases. When we were finally released without charge, we faced a barrage of cameras and reporters. I noticed the son of a friend of mine was in the crowd, grinning from ear to ear. He had been arguing with his father about tactics like occupations, and here was a friend of his father's pulling off the kind of direct action he supported.

255

When my eyes connected with his, he gave me the thumbs-up and my feelings flooded back into my chest. When I told the media why we did this as Jewish women, my anguish over the situation of the people of Gaza was obvious. That clip was picked up by Al Jazeera Arabic TV and ran with a headline that translates as, "Jewish Women Protest Gaza Attack." A Palestinian friend told me later that it did more to combat anti-Semitism in the Middle East than any action he'd ever seen.

I can still dissociate when I'm in a crisis, but I try to avoid such situations as much as possible because now I feel the price my body and my mind will pay. For a couple of years after, I paid for the action at the Israeli consulate with PTSD symptoms like flashbacks, but in this case it was worth it.

I FEEL GRATEFUL to my five-year-old self for having the imagination, the courage, and the tenacity to split off from the unbearable horrors inflicted upon her by the man who was supposed to protect her. She created heroes who protected her from the knowledge that might have driven her mad and certainly would have made her dysfunctional.

I don't see multiple personality disorder as a disorder at all. I think it's a brilliant defence mechanism that a child who experiences severe trauma without help can employ. The alters helped me not only survive but thrive in many ways. Given my economic and social privilege, I think the abuse I suffered and my need to face my fragmented personality helped me be a better activist, one who could understand multiple realities faced by people in different circumstances due to colonialism, racism, patriarchy, and capitalism. When I told my friend Donna Mergler, a brilliant neurophysiologist, about my personalities she said, "My god, you have a beautiful brain, Judy." I think we all have a beautiful brain but sometimes trauma provokes extraordinary creativity as well as extraordinary destruction. Understanding that helps me understand how much creativity and energy is lost to the world because we marginalize people labelled "mentally ill."

Without my brother Alvin, I don't think I would have survived. He has always been with me, even when things were very difficult. He has taught me what family can be, and in the process we, along with my brother Leonard, have healed our family so the new generation of beautiful, loved, and lovely children will not suffer from the injuries that were inflicted upon us. It was my mother's dying wish that we stay together and we have.

I have learned to love and even to accept love. I've learned to trust and am now much more open-hearted and emotional — sometimes too emotional, but that might also be age. I'm still single, and in my seventies likely to stay that way.

I almost never feel alone anymore. Of course I never was.

ACKNOWLEDGEMENTS

A LOT OF PEOPLE helped me write this book. This memoir is very different from the other books I have written and I had to learn to write in a new way. It has taken me eight years to complete it, with a lot of help from editors, friends, and comrades.

Janie Yoon, my editor at House of Anansi, put up with my resistance to deleting some of my favourite stories to produce what I hope is a well-crafted story of the most important part of my life. Her patience, determination, kindness, and skill served me well and I am very grateful.

Almost a decade ago, Wayson Choy, my teacher at the Humber Writer's School summer program, encouraged me to write a memoir based on a single story I wrote for his class.

My old friend Bob Chodos generously helped me with editing throughout the process. Friends Derrick O'Keefe and Cynthia Flood kindly gave me feedback on early drafts of the book. My former editor Barbara Pulling provided helpful feedback on a first draft. Karen Connolly, through the Humber College Creative Writing by Correspondence course, gave me invaluable instruction that transformed the book. And friends Susan Swan, Sheila Heti, Mike Hoolboom, and Corvin Russell gave me feedback and support on a later draft.

Halfway through the process I worked with a stellar writers' group that included b. h. Yael, Suzanne Weiss, Jacob Scheier, and Phil Hébert. Willa Marcus generously examined the text with a legal eye.

I am deeply grateful to the Canada Council for the Arts for providing me with a mid-career writing grant in 2012 that helped me make the transition from professor, journalist, and activist to full-time writer, and to the Banff Centre for Arts and Creativity for offering me a supportive space that allowed me to delve into difficult memories.

Next I must thank my agent Samantha Haywood, who took me on even though she was so busy, and sold the book with great integrity and transparency.

Before I started working on this version of my life, I interviewed a lot of people, many of whom don't appear in these pages. They know who they are and I thank them, as well as the people who made it despite the many cuts.

To my friends, new and old, who have given me much support through what was sometimes a very difficult process, please know that I couldn't have done it without you.

To my family, who are the most important people in my life. They have always had to put up with my public profile, but revealing your family secrets is very difficult, especially when you are not the one telling the secrets.

GLOSSARY

ASL: American Sign Language

CARAL: Canadian Association for Repeal of the Abortion Law

CAW: Canadian Auto Workers

CHS: Canadian Hearing Society

IWD: International Women's Day

LEAF: Legal Education Action Fund

LSA: League for Socialist Action

NAC: National Action Committee on the Status of Women

OCAC: Ontario Coalition for Abortion Clinics

RMG: Revolutionary Marxist Group

RWL: Revolutionary Workers League

SDS: Students for a Democratic Society

TAC: Therapeutic Abortion Committee

NOTES

PROLOGUE: WARRIOR WOMAN

Cheryl was behind him: Vicki Russell, "Henry Morgentaler attacked at abortion clinic opening," *The National*, aired June 15, 1983, http://www.cbc.ca/archives/entry/morgentaler-attacked-at-clinic-opening.

CHAPTER 1: THE WALL COMES DOWN

Dodd told the *Toronto Star*: Stephen Bindman, "Dodd Calls Abortion Fight Her 'Biggest Humiliation,'" *Toronto Star*. Toronto, Ontario: July 13, 1989, p.1.

CHAPTER 5: "IT WAS McGILL THAT RUINED YOU"

Laura Sabia speech: Judy Rebick, *McGill Daily*. Montreal, QC: November 6, 1964.

The charge against him was: Joy Fenston, *McGill Daily*. Montreal, QC: November 9, 1965.

CHAPTER 12: THE CLINIC WILL STAY OPEN

Morris Manning's summary to jury: Kirk Makin, "Acquitting
Morgentaler Called Invitation to Anarchy," *Globe and Mail*.
Toronto, ON: November 3, 1984.

Chief Justice Brian Dickson wrote: "Abortion Rights: Significant
Moments in Canadian History," CBC News. Toronto, ON: January
13, 2009. Available at http://www.cbc.ca/news/canada/abortion-
rights-significant-moments-in-canadian-history-1.787212.

CHAPTER 13: SOMETHING'S HAPPENING HERE

Studies find that 19 to 28 percent: Bessel van der Kolk, MD, *The
Body Keeps the Score: Brain, Mind, and Body in the Healing of
Trauma* (New York: Viking, 2014), p. 190.

Dissociation is the essence: Ibid.

The American Psychiatric Association defines: The American
Psychiatric Association's definition of dissociative identity disorder is available at https://www.psychiatry.org/patients-families/
dissociative-disorders/what-are-dissociative-disorders.

CHAPTER 15: AND THEN THERE WERE NINE

February 21, 1990: Journal entries appear exactly as they are written, including grammatical mistakes.

CHAPTER 16: THROWING CAUTION TO THE WIND

We barged up the stairs: Cheryl Cornacchia, "Rebel with many
causes; 'Radical' Judy Rebick brings fire to women's movement,"
The Gazette. Montreal, QC: July 6, 1990.

The women's movement has returned: Ibid.

CHAPTER 18: THE BEST OF TIMES

The *Toronto Star* headline: David Vienneaum, "Proposed rape law's message: No means no," *Toronto Star*. Toronto, ON: November 21, 1991.

CHAPTER 19: THE FINAL CONFRONTATION

After the final conference in Vancouver: Michele Landsberg, "Women send fresh message on Constitution to smug leaders," *Toronto Star*. Toronto, ON: February 21, 1992.

INDEX

Author photograph: Courtesy Ben Holbrook/National Speakers Bureau

JUDY REBICK is a well-known social justice and feminist activist, writer, journalist, educator, and speaker. She is the author of *Transforming Power: From the Personal to the Political, Occupy This!, Ten Thousand Roses: The Making of a Feminist Revolution*, and *Imagine Democracy*, and the co-author of *Politically Speaking*, with Kiké Roach. Founding publisher of rabble.ca, Canada's popular independent online news and discussion site, Judy continues to blog there. She is a former president of the National Action Committee on the Status of Women, Canada's largest women's group, and was the first CAW–Sam Gindin Chair in Social Justice and Democracy at Ryerson University. During the 1990s, she was the host of two national TV shows on CBC *Newsworld* and is now a frequent commentator on CBC Radio and Television. In the 1980s, she was a well-known spokesperson for the pro-choice movement during the fight to legalize abortion. She lives in Toronto.